— *panic* —
PROOF

How the Right Virtual Assistant Can
Save Your Sanity and Grow Your Business

by
Jess Ostroff

Never forget rule #1: DON'T PANIC!
Jess Ostroff

This book is dedicated my mom, my dad, and Andy. You've taught me that sometimes (okay, most of the time) patience is a virtue, that perseverance means never letting the jerks get in your way, and that there are no can'ts and no won'ts in this great game called life. I've never once doubted that you have my back, even when I take big risks and make stupid decisions. I wouldn't be here without you, so thank you.
I love you.

This book is also dedicated to all the terrible, no-good, very bad clients who tried to poison me over the course of my career as a virtual assistant. Guess what? I found the antidote and it's within the pages of this book!

TABLE OF CONTENTS

Rule #3: Don't Drive the Bus, Co-Pilot the Plane

FOREWORD

by Ann Handley

I was sitting at my desk. It was early Sunday morning.

I know it was a Sunday because I remember how sorry for myself I felt. And that sorrow had everything to do with the fact that I was sitting at my desk. On a Sunday morning.

The rest of the world was at brunch or sleeping in or preparing the Sunday roast or doing all the fabulous and fun weekend things I suddenly imagined myself doing—if I weren't sitting at my desk that moment.

Yet again.

I love my job. To even call it a "job" is a little weird, because like a lot of execs I don't really separate out "work" time the way the typical 9-to-5er might. It's not a job—it's who I am.

I don't mind the weekends or evenings. But for many months I'd spent weekends and evenings grappling with all the details, minutiae, and particulars I couldn't seem to get to otherwise.

So that Sunday morning, sitting there at my desk, I was at a breaking point—mostly because of the consistent volume.

Said another way: *All my (little) time + all the (many) things = Wallowing in a deep pool of self-pitying sorrow*

I turned to our collective oracle and, it would turn out, my savior: Google's search field. And from my keyboard tumbled something incoherent like this:

OVERWHELMED NEED HELP NOW EXECUTIVE ASSISTANT VIRTUAL

Google delivered a company called Don't Panic Management. (*Too late!* I remember thinking. *I'm already panicking!*)

The voice on the Don't Panic homepage was specific and soothing:

"Are you overwhelmed with handling details that are distracting you from the things you're good at?" *Check.*

"Do you need help with calendaring? Content curation? Writing? Research? Life details?" *Yes.*

"Are you crying with relief right now?" *I AM.*

"Do you need a hug?" *Nods head vigorously, unable to speak from lump in throat.*

And just like that, I felt the pool of sorrow start to evaporate a little.

Jess and I talked the next day. I hired her on the spot.

She became my assistant, my life organizer, my right-hand Jess. She has helped me up my game in immeasurable ways.

She solves problems. She reads my mind. She proactively delivers what I haven't even said I need. She has helped restore balance to what was quickly becoming unsustainable.

That was 20 years ago. And the rest is history.

*

Jess is going to edit this and fix everything. She's going to tell me that we'd actually met at an event prior to my teary Sunday-morning googling.

She's going to inform me that the words on her company's homepage didn't read exactly as I remember. There were zero hugs proffered.

She's going to remind me that I didn't hire her on the spot: It took a few days for her to put a proposal together.

And this whole thing definitely *was not* 20 years ago . . . because Jess would've been . . . uh, in grade school? It was actually 5 years ago, just after my first book came out, and just around the time I was contemplating the second.

But the gist of the story is true. The core is sound. The substance of what she provides is all there. Even *if* the specific details—of this story and of my life—are . . . well, better left to Jess.

All those years ago I thought I needed an admin to sort out the details. But what I ultimately got was much better: I got a partner who helps me in innumerable ways. I got someone I can trust.

Jess has my back, always. But she also gives me a shove when I need it. She offers advice. She adds value. She thinks about things I miss: Because even while she's focused on the details, she somehow also sees the bigger picture.

I don't know how she does that. Magic, maybe.

And that's what I wish for you. That in reading Jess's book you get a better sense of what you need in your own virtual assistant.

The assisting is the easy part: You probably already have a mental list of tasks that need doing. But it's the other things—the trust, the relationship, the *partners-in-crime vibe*—that this book can help you identify, articulate, and find.

I don't even know you. And yet I suspect you need all that.

Honestly, who doesn't?

Ann Handley
Chief Content Officer, MarketingProfs
Wall Street Journal bestselling author
Lucky client of Jess

PROLOGUE

I'm in a small house in the woods of New Hampshire. The sun is pouring into my borrowed office where I've got a lime La Croix and a cup of fresh French Press coffee because I'm that annoying millennial who accidentally follows trends. (Hey, if it's good, why not?)

There's a lake down the road a few steps, but I can't see it from where I'm sitting, which is probably for the best because I'm not here to float aimlessly under the soft, pillowy clouds.

No, I have tucked myself into a remote environment without wifi (the horror, I know!) because I decided it was time for me to do something terrifying. Something that I had been wanting to do for years:

Write this book.

The ideas have been floating around in my head for ages now and they're ready to come tumbling onto the page.

So here I am, taking a short sabbatical from my real life. It feels strange to be here, in the middle of July, on this small, eight-day retreat in the woods, cut off from internet, staring at green. Green trees. Green grass. I even have a green mug.

I've never taken time off from my daily work and life responsibilities to do something that didn't directly and immediately impact the bottom line of the business. I've never jumped off the deep end to work on a project that was risky and had an unknown outcome.

"But you're an entrepreneur!" I say to myself. "You're taking risks every day!"

"Not really, self. I do what I know. I do what I'm good at. In fact, I'd argue that I'm more of a risk-mitigator, not a risk-taker. You know this!" I remind myself. Even though starting a business is always risky, I did it in the safest way possible. (More on that later.)

But writing a book? That's something new. And new things are scary. And I don't like scary things. And I've certainly never gone this long without checking email . . . oh god, what is in that inbox right now??

Focus, Jess. Deep breaths. The inbox can wait.

I am never without a device and I have an email-checking compulsion. I'm a passionate and fun-loving ambivert who loves to work hard and play harder.

Even when I'm on vacation I check in. There's something about going through and organizing my emails every day that makes me feel safe and whole. Perhaps you can relate?

Because, you see, I'm an entrepreneur, which means that I like solving problems. I like helping people. That's what keeps me up all day (and all night). It's what makes me tick, what floats my boat, what puts a shimmy in my step. So, clearly, I must be aware of all of the problems all of the time so that I can be available to solve them.

Come here, problems! I need to fix you!

It's a madness that I'm not particularly proud of.

But that's not all. I'm a manager. I'm a productivity nerd. I'm a musician. I'm a chef. I'm a servant. I'm a writer.

Writing to help you find your own place of calm—your own retreat during which to do the things you have always wanted to do. To help you avoid the mistakes I made when growing and scaling a business. And, ultimately, to help you celebrate the greatness of work and life every way you can.

I have to admit, I never thought I would be here. When I graduated from New York University's Stern School of Business, I had no idea how to use my shiny new marketing and international business degree. My allergy to corporate America led me to apply for an AmeriCorps program in Los Angeles. It was easily the hardest year of my life. I saw a life of poverty, of violence, and of an unimaginable language and cultural barrier right here in my own country.

Applying myself to a year of service was as grueling as it was fulfilling. I learned that I could indeed work for 12 hours a day, every day, and stay standing when it was over. I learned that I could survive being constantly berated in a language I didn't understand. I learned that I could live on $800 per month. I learned that food stamps worked at Trader Joe's (#winning).

I learned that if I could make it through that, I could probably make it through anything.

When I graduated from AmeriCorps, I applied the ~$5,000 Education Award to my student loan balance (hell yes) and found a position as a social media coordinator at a nonprofit. Now, this was 2009. Social media wasn't exactly a "thing" yet, although Twitter and Facebook existed and people were networking online, learning online, and finding and using websites consistently.

I was tasked with building out a digital marketing plan for a new high school leadership program. I got to use my organizational and marketing skills to create something that would benefit students, and thus, change the world. This was the perfect fit for me to combine my college degree and my dedication to service.

Of course, it's never that simple, right? I quickly found myself being bound by red tape, cranky graphic designers, and a boss who didn't know what "social media" even was.

That's when I decided to use some of my free time to build upon my own social networks.

Twitter was the latest and greatest at the time. I set up an account, followed a few news outlets, and came across a former internship boss, @jaybaer. When I worked for him, Jay was the head of all things digital at an agency. Since then, I learned, he had moved on to start a digital marketing consultancy and advisory firm.

And holy crap, Jay had a lot of followers! He was actually *doing* the social media thing for a living—and doing it well.

It was fortuitous timing when I saw a tweet from Jay that said this:

Oooooooohhhhh!

What's a virtual assistant? I asked myself. A quick Google search told me that it was just what it sounded like: an assistant who worked virtually.

To me, that meant that anything that could be done online or with a computer was fair game in virtual assistant land, and boy, was I excited about that!

I stared longingly out of my cubicle window. At the time, my office was less than a mile from the California coast. I wanted to go there. Was it possible that I could work wherever I wanted for someone who actually knew what he was doing? Were my skills and experience right for this sort of thing? Could my passion for making a difference be combined with my need for paying the bills?

I had to find out. So, I responded to his tweet and then sent an email.

*

"Hi boss," I wrote, hoping for some brownie points. I had no idea what I would say to convince him to hire me, but I placed my bets on some good old Ostroff wit and charm. I won't bore you with the contents of the entire email, but I will tell you that I thought it was a good idea to list the top seven reasons why he should hire me to be his virtual assistant. One of them was that I was a fellow tequila-lover.

What was I thinking? I cringe. . .

But he hired me! And the rest is history! That's the end!

Just kidding.

A glimpse of my future came into focus. I was booking flights, researching blog post ideas, calling the Sonic on the side of the highway where Jay left his wallet on the way to the airport, and I was doing it on my own time, with my own resources, and all via email. Can you imagine? I barely had to talk to anyone on the phone, let alone in person. It was an extroverted introvert's dream!

Here's what Jay had to say about the whole situation:

> *Before I sent that tweet, I'd always been pretty darn self-reliant. I'd had several executive positions and all that, but had never had an administrative assistant. I guess I always felt like I could do it faster and better myself. (Boy was that stupid!) But when I started Convince & Convert, I essentially started back at zero with no clients and zero dollars of income. I had to build everything from scratch, and I realized marketing and communications was shifting to be more about a bunch of little things vs. a few big things. I needed HELP.*
>
> *I really didn't know what a virtual assistant was or what they did. I just knew I needed an "assistant" and since I worked from home and wasn't keen to be sharing my guest room every day with someone else, that assistant needed to be "virtual." I didn't have a good sense for duties, or what I should pay, or how to communicate or manage a VA. But, I figured I'd just put it out there on Twitter and see what happened. And BAM, Jess came back into my life. Now, 10 years later, my life is totally different (and way better) as a result.*

Lucky for me, Jay is an extremely generous guy, as you can see. He knew he only needed about ten hours of my time each week, but he didn't want to risk losing me because I couldn't make ends meet with only ten hours per week. He referred me to several friends and colleagues who were starting their own businesses or consulting agencies at the time. And remember, that time was rough. The economic collapse in 2008 left many people without work, or at the very least rethinking what they wanted to do and who they wanted to be in the world.

A terrible time for many of the working class. A wonderful time for a budding virtual assistant.

To say that my life completely changed thanks to that tweet feels like the understatement of the year and doesn't begin to capture all the amazing things Jay has done for me. This was the start to my new career and I can't thank Jay enough. He went out on a limb and supported me endlessly during a time when I barely knew how to use Google Docs and he continues to support my business as a client, colleague, and friend today. Love you, Jay!

Anywhoozle, as soon as I had enough client hours to pay my rent and buy a few things at Trader Joe's, I put in my two weeks' notice. When I made up my mind about something not being right for me, I was firm in making a change. And quickly.

I navigated the treacherous waters of work-from-home life with ease. I could wake up early and get my work done before spending a few hours at the beach. Or I could put in a solid eight hours before 3 p.m. so I could beat traffic to visit friends in Los Feliz. (If you have ever lived or spent time in L.A., you understand the soul-sucking burden of planning your life around traffic.)

Sometimes, I felt lost. Was this my life now? Was I making enough of a difference for people?

My mom sent me job postings from The New York Times. She was thinking:

Why did we send our daughter to NYU and spend all this money for her to do something that I don't even know what it is? What's virtual? What's a virtual assistant? Even now when I tell people things about what she does, people ask if she's some kind of alien.

My friends from college thought I was catching waves and frolicking along the beach day in and day out.

No one back home had any idea how I made money.

But I knew what I was doing. I was living a life that I designed quite literally from scratch. I was living my passion for freedom. For location-independence. For not always doing what everyone else told me to do. For taking pride in the work that I did.

And for helping someone else live their best life at the same time.

Cut to today, over eight years later, and it's become apparent that this virtual workforce isn't just a flash in the pan. It's the wave of the future.

The number of telecommuting employees increased by 80 percent between 2005 and 2012 and that number continues to climb in 2018 and beyond[1].

---

1. Global Workplace Analytics. "2017 State of Telecommuting in the U.S." Global Workplace Analytics, globalworkplaceanalytics.com/telecommuting-statistics.

Richard Branson says[1] that "one day offices will be a thing of the past."

Freelancers now account for 34 percent of the total US workforce[2]. Surveys of global leaders worldwide say they predict that half the workforce will be working virtually by 2020[3].

These numbers didn't resonate with me at the time since I was one of the only people I knew who was doing this sort of work. And I thought I'd be working a location-independent job, maintaining my "work hard, play hard" mentality, and choosing a life I built by myself forever.

The difference between my original plan and what actually came to fruition was that I accidentally built a company.

As someone who billed hourly for services, I foolishly overlooked the major downfall in the model: there are only so many hours in a day. So, even if I continued to

---

1. Branson, Richard. "One day offices will be a thing of the past." Virgin, 27 Apr. 2017, www.virgin.com/richard-branson/one-day-offices-will-be-a-thing-of-the-past.

2. Edelman Berland. "Freelancing in America: A National Survey of the New Workforce." Freelancers Union and Elance-oDesk, 4 Sept. 2014, fu-web-storage-prod. s3.amazonaws.com/content/filer_public/7c/45/7c457488-0740-4bc4-ae45-0aa60daac531/freelancinginamerica_ report.pdf.

3. Vanderkam, Laura. "Will Half Of People Be Working Remotely By 2020?" Fast Company, 14 Aug. 2014, www. fastcompany.com/3034286/will-half-of-people-be-working-remotely-by-2020.

contract more work, I would only be able to do so much on my own.

Don't Panic Management, my budding virtual assistant agency, was born because my workload outgrew my capacity. Plain and simple.

Over the years, we've grown and evolved more than I ever could have imagined or planned for. (Business plans be damned!) And today, I like to say that my team and I are not just virtual assistants. We're something more.

In the best relationships, we become partners in our clients' businesses. We have a seat at the table when it comes to making strategic decisions because we're in the weeds of the day-to-day projects that allow their businesses to run smoothly.

We are able to get inside our clients' heads and determine their needs often before they even realize them. We're able to make decisions on their behalf when they're overwhelmed and overworked. We're their right-hand workhorses, providing useful services with a smile and a high five.

And we have the opportunity to play a role in leading innovation for this industry.

Assisting people in their scheduling and content marketing isn't what I planned to be doing with my life per se, but making a difference while earning enough money to support my own lifestyle is. And the only way I knew how to do that was by offering a digital hand to entrepreneurs and managers in need.

As it turns out, this little business that could has changed more than just the lives of our clients. Among our ranks, we have team members pursuing their dreams, growing their families, and living their ideal lifestyles as we help clients achieve their goals.

In conversations over the years and throughout my travels, I've learned that there are many, many other people out there who have the same basic needs as I do: being useful at work, going on adventures, and finding community.

So, how do we provide these opportunities to more people? How can I help you further develop the skills you already have and delegate the ones you don't? How can your business grow effectively with all of the benefits and none of the migraines?

That's my goal for this book. It's my hope that by equipping you with the tools and resources you need to understand and develop a successful virtual assistant relationship, you'll be able to create the business you've always wanted while providing a sustainable and fulfilling life for a wonderful person at the same time.

INTRODUCTION

The conversation around virtual assistants has gone from terrible to just "meh" in the last ten years. This is progress, but it's not exactly inspiring. What started as a cheap way to get a few things done for executives and entrepreneurs is finally being taken seriously by more than just the early adopters.

It's finally not just me telling everyone that virtual assistants can grow businesses and change lives. Yeehaw!

Yet the positive elements that virtual assistants can bring to the table don't always outshine the negatives when it comes to common perceptions, unfortunately.

As a virtual assistant myself, I've spoken to all kinds of other VAs across the globe. At one point or another, every assistant I've spoken with, including myself, has felt a sense of discrimination or a feeling of "lesser than." Maybe it's related to the old movies and stories we hear about assistant-executive relationships. One gives the orders and the other one follows.

I think we can all agree that *Mad Men*-style model of client and assistant relationships is a thing of the past, or at least it should be. Today's assistants come in all experience-levels, genders, shapes, and sizes (we can't all be Joan Holloway after all!), but some of the stereotypes around assistant capabilities are, sadly, still prevalent.

Perhaps the fact that VAs don't get to interact with clients face-to-face on a daily basis magnifies the idea that we don't have to treat assistants like real human beings. Maybe we've never managed someone before and don't know how. Or maybe the idea that a virtual assistant is more than a faceless data nerd is entirely unimaginable.

I'm not sure why this industry is so stuck in the past. But the treatment of assistants like dim-witted lemmings is all too common. For example:

Sending vague instructions and expecting our assistants to "figure it out."

Negotiating the crap out of rates (over email, by the way, not via phone or video conference) to undercut their value.

Sending passive aggressive text messages about issues instead of providing real, concrete feedback.

Providing necessary materials at the last minute, or whenever it's convenient for us, so that our assistants have to scramble to meet deadlines.

I hate to break the news, but guess what? These kinds of virtual assistants, the human beings you're interacting with, don't live in the cloud. They're NOT the Alexas or the Siris or the Cortanas of the world.

They are real people.

And the second we stop treating VAs as second-class citizens is the second that VAs can begin to truly thrive as change-makers. *Because that's what VAs are.*

Many of the best VAs I've worked with care more about their clients than they do about themselves. They sacrifice early mornings, late evenings, and weekends for the sake of making their clients' businesses more successful. It's useful for the client because, in many cases, VAs are in charge of schedules. They set systems. They have all the behind-the-scenes knowledge that keeps the trains running on time. They will do everything in their power to make sure their clients are happy.

The clients we see the most success with at Don't Panic Management are the ones who have fully integrated their VA into their daily work and life. Their VAs are a part of the planning process and are aware of the company's goals so that both the client and the VA can reach toward them together. VAs are cherished gems and clients can't imagine life without them.

One successful example is a gal who we matched with a client who had all kinds of different needs. From inbox management to copywriting, podcast production to project management, we weren't sure if there was going to be one person who "had it all" in this scenario.

Normally, when faced with a client who has the need for multiple different services, we assign two or three assistants and then manage them internally so the client isn't faced with more work. In this case, and in more and more cases that I see each day, clients want one beautiful unicorn to handle it all.

The reason that's possible now is because eager, curious virtual assistants will take the skills they've learned over time and their can-do attitudes and apply them to new challenges. Even though this particular VA had no clue about how to produce a podcast, she wanted to learn, and so she did.

When I was worried that managing the client's email inbox was below her, she proved me wrong. She loved the variety of tasks and appreciated a change of pace from performing her daily marketing duties. The client would probably steal her and keep her in their back pocket if we let them. (I would love to keep her in my pocket, too, actually. She is just delightful!)

This is the ideal scenario. You want to work with someone who cares about getting work done just as much as you do. Unfortunately, this isn't the case with every assistant, so it's up to you to be extra careful. And as an industry, we have a long way to go before all virtual assistants share the same amazing persistence, curiosity, and expertise that many of the best assistants possess.

Fortunately, you've taken the first step toward helping us change the virtual assistant landscape by reading this book. Go you!

Now, if you're thinking, "Wait a second! That's not me! I don't even know what a VA is! I just want to figure out what they are and whether I need one! Give me a break!" That's okay! There are three books that came out between 2013 and 2014 that are important in building up the role of the virtual assistant and how it can positively impact businesses. If you aren't already convinced about the basics and benefits of getting virtual help, you may want to start there:

- *Virtual Freedom* by Chris Ducker (hi, Chris!!)
- *The Virtual Assistant Solution* by Michael Hyatt
- *Virtual Assistant Assistant* by Nick Loper

There are lots of others out there, but these were, and continue to be, the most popular books on the subject. Chris, Michael, and Nick also write about hiring, working with, and building a thriving business using virtual assistants on their own sites. (Chris, in particular, is in a unique position because he runs a virtual assistant company out of the Philippines.)

I mention these books because I want you to have some other resources for working with VAs if you don't like mine or simply aren't ready for it. They all have a slightly different take, but all provide hands-on strategies for helping you understand why it's important to hire a VA. I think they're a great place to start for a lot of people.

I also want to mention these folks because I'm sharing ideas and strategies from a very specific and different perspective than these folks:

I am both a virtual assistant AND an entrepreneur who manages a team of virtual assistants.

I can see the advantages and disadvantages from both sides. I can share stories from down deep in the weeds, and I can tell you what it really feels like to work with someone just like you.

And, as a result, I'm going to be dropping truth bombs on you left and right. You may not like that. I understand, believe me. It ain't easy trying something new, or, perhaps, breaking bad habits. But the sooner you do, the better off you'll be.

Here are some things I'm *not* going to do in this book (that you can get from other books, including the ones listed above):

- Tell you how much your time is worth
- Tell you why you need help
- Convince you that you shouldn't do everything yourself
- Convince you that you need to hire a VA

I am assuming that you:

- Know you might be ready for some help (you're panicking!)
- Know that time is quite literally money
- Know one or two things about the existence of virtual assistants

What I *will* help you with is:

- How to dig deep into finding the things you love to do so you can do more of them
- How to determine whether you need an executive assistant, a virtual assistant, or something else
- How to become super aware about who you are as a person, what kind of manager you are, and what your needs are
- Why soft skills matter more than hard skills
- What core values you should look for in a virtual assistant
- How to find, interview, and test a VA
- What to include in a contract that protects both you and your VA
- The most common mistakes clients make when starting to work with a VA
- The most common mistakes VAs make (and how to spot them before they become a problem for you)
- How to not be a terrible, horrible, no good, very bad client
- How to nurture your VA to create a relationship based on trust, strong communication, and long-term success
- How you're building a future of world-changers by contributing to the virtual economy

And of course, I'll give you some fun, real-life examples to show you how it all works in action. Here are the rules of the road. If you follow them closely, I promise your life will change.

Hopefully for the better.

Rule #1:

DON'T PANIC

chapter one

TIME TO TAKE OFF THAT SUPERHERO COSTUME

"Superhero Syndrome" is not a well-known phrase. In fact, I can't remember where I first learned about it. Since I've become acquainted with it, however, I find myself noticing elements of this elusive syndrome all around me.

Let's take its definition to start. Raise your hand if any of these statements sound familiar:

I feel like I can do it all (and have it all).

I need to be everything to everyone.

If I don't finish everything on my list, I feel like a failure.

I often say yes when I really want to say no.

If you raised your hand to even one of these, you might be suffering from your own bout of Superhero Syndrome.

I know what this feels like because all of these statements resemble me, just a few years ago.

The year was 2014. I had been working remotely and living my best life since 2010. My little LLC was growing with increasing velocity. People were starting to actually "get" what I did for work. (My mom stopped sending me job postings from The New York Times. Finally!) I had hired my first full-time employee to help me manage my clients' needs.

This was a big deal. My little business was proving to be successful, something people truly wanted. According to my entrepreneurship classes in college, the best entrepreneurs find a need and then they fill it. I was really doing that!

But instead of feeling proud and accomplished, I felt sick.

Every morning I'd wake up in a panic, worrying about whatever email I forgot to send last night, what meeting I had to get ready for, and all the other tasks I was probably already behind on. I would frantically run from my bed to my desk like Miley Cyrus swinging on a wrecking ball and, let me tell you from experience, that's not a good way to start your day.

In the spring of that year, I went on a west coast road trip for "vacation." This was the first time I turned off email notifications on my phone. (I didn't remove the email app like many people do because that was

TERRIFYING.) I thought I was supposed to relax, so I did my best not to check on things, but instead of providing me with a sense of calm, the unknown filled me with a sense of dread.

Within a week of returning home, I was at the urgent care center because my throat was on fire and I was so tired and nauseated that I couldn't work.

That was the only time I would drag myself to a doctor: when I physically could not sit or lay in bed with my laptop and do work.

I had an incredibly rough bout of strep throat that my physician said she hadn't seen in years. She asked, "So, how are you feeling?" "Not great," I replied. "Yeah, I don't know what took you so long to come over here. Your throat looks NASTY!" Thanks.

A month later, I was sitting in my favorite pizza restaurant enjoying a lovely Sunday evening dinner when the sharpest pain radiated up to my shoulder and down to my ankle. I couldn't walk and had to get in a cab immediately to make the ten blocks home.

This case of sciatica left me incapacitated for a week. For a while after that, I could only be standing straight up or lying flat, so I fashioned a makeshift stand-up desk out of a Crock-Pot box and a pile of records. As you do.

(I promptly got in trouble for the records thing and moved them. Apparently you're not supposed to lie them flat like this. I SHOULD HAVE KNOWN!)

A few months later, I felt a tingle and then some flu-like symptoms followed by major itching, burning, and pain on the right side of my head. (I'm noticing a pattern with all this right-side mumbo jumbo, aren't you? Maybe because I'm a lefty? Who knows?)

I did the thing again where I tried to get through it on my own, didn't take any time off, and finally went to the clinic when I could barely see and couldn't sleep because of the pain.

"Looks like an allergic reaction," they told me. "Take some Zyrtec and a nap."

If you've learned anything from this string of events so far, you know that the stupid Zyrtec didn't work. I finally went to a dermatologist a few days later when the pain became unbearable. She said she couldn't be sure, because this was not a standard presentation, but thought perhaps it was shingles.

THE SHINGLES.

I was 28 years old and I had shingles. My brain was swimming around thousands of questions and frantic thoughts including: "But, but, but aren't I healthy? Isn't this something that weak immune systems are prone to? How in the world is this happening right now??"

And also: "Thank all the gourmet cheese plates in the world that it's not bed bugs!" (I thought it could be anything at the time!)

Once I picked my jaw up off the floor, got myself to a pharmacy, and started taking the meds, things healed quickly. I could feel some relief within a day and was back to full energy within two weeks.

As I spoke to friends and family about it, they told me their stories of friends' experiences and even their own struggles with the virus. If the cause wasn't a result of a compromised immune system related to another condition or illness, it was because of a traumatic or stressful event.

"What was my event?" I kept thinking to myself. I couldn't place it. There was no death in the family, no divorce, no big move, and no job change. The traditional stressors that give people heart palpitations were not in my life at the time. So, I kept going.

Meanwhile, my right knee, which had been operated on in 2000, started bothering me again. Because why wouldn't an injury from 14 years ago flare up for no apparent reason just when everything else starts crumbling as well?

Because I couldn't admit to myself that I am not, in fact, a superhero.

My Harry Potter Scar

By the end of 2014, I had a lot of rehab exercises to keep up with, a ton of sleep to catch up on, and a scar on my forehead just right of center. These days, my bangs tend to cover it. Most people don't notice it.

But I know it's there.

And when I'm feeling particularly panicky, I touch it. Because it's my reminder. It's my Harry Potter scar. It's the thing that tells me that he-who-must-not-be-named is still out there plotting his revenge if I let him.

It was around this time, toward the end of 2014, when I figured out my "event." My Voldemort. It didn't happen all at once. It was a lifetime of pushing myself to be independent, to complete every project, to live my best life, to work hard and play harder . . . to do it all. I was always an overachiever. And by that point I had developed the Superhero Syndrome where not only did I think I could do everything, I thought that if I handed anything off to someone else that I was an utter disappointment in life.

I wore busy like a badge of honor. I thought that running feverishly from one commitment to the next was the right way to live. And I thought that if I wasn't filling my life with projects and to-do lists then I wasn't doing it right (life, that is).

I'm sure your story looks different than mine. Perhaps it wasn't the shingles, but a sudden onset of depression. Or something a little more minor, like forgetting to pick up the kid from soccer practice again because you were stuck deep in your inbox, sending last-minute invoices, or trying to troubleshoot with a client.

Or maybe you're waking up at 3 a.m., night after night, suddenly remembering that thing you forgot to do yesterday and scurrying over to your laptop to make it happen.

Maybe your significant other is PISSED because you can't get through date night without a "client emergency." (They will never understand.)

No matter what it is, you're here because you've got a problem. A pain that needs healing. An itch that needs scratching.

And I get it because I was there.

I was ruining vacations with emails that HAD to be addressed. I was up in the middle of the night clamoring to my desk because I accidentally left something in draft mode instead of published. Or forgot to mark an expense. Or pay a tax bill.

I was panicking. All. The. Time.

Which is frankly ridiculous given that I started a company called Don't Panic Management. You see, that naming convention was just as much for me as it was for everyone else that wanted to work with me.

I was the nervous nellie who was overworked (and underpaid). I was the micromanager and the control freak on a lifelong quest to fill every moment with hard work and hard play.

At the same time, I was also the one whose body rebelled and simply said, "NOPE!"

Sometimes it takes a rebellious body to force you to take it down a notch and to reevaluate whether all the things you're doing are really working. And this rude awakening made me realize that my business is built on human beings, that my brain and my hands and my fingers are what make the projects get done day in and day out, and that if those things don't work, the business doesn't work.

Underneath it all, I was ultimately unaware of what my body and mind needed to sustain themselves in a healthy way so I could work and live. As a result, my business suffered. If I wasn't going to get healthy for myself, I was going to get healthy for my business.

Because isn't that the other side of the Superhero Syndrome coin? We will do anything for other people, but we won't spend one second doing something for ourselves.

The first step to overcoming stress, anxiety, and burnout is to not panic. You will get through this. But you can't possibly get through it if you can't find a way to take a deep breath.

chapter two

DO WHAT YOU LOVE (OR AT LEAST WHAT YOU LIKE)

One of the only ways I was able to get out of my Cycle of Sick, as I like to call it, was to stop. Stop working. Stop planning things. Stop scheduling myself into oblivion.

Stopping, as you can imagine, was not easy for someone whose two basic states of being were working and sleeping, with nothing in between. But it was the only way I could find the time to evaluate what was going on, or perhaps more importantly, what wasn't going on, so I could get back on track.

I had to do a little soul searching. Light the candles and commence the yoga breathing, everybody! If you've got a yurt in your backyard, pull back the hide and let us in!

Now is a good time for me to be clear about something, lest your brow furrowed at the mere mention of "yoga": This is not a self-help book. And I'm not a psychologist. So if you need that sort of thing, I highly recommend you get a good therapist (or even a great business coach) and also read the book *Get Your Sh*t Together* by Sarah Knight.

(Sarah's wit, humor, and candid style was part of what inspired me to write this book, by the way, so big shout out to Sarah!)

Instead of prescribing you a meditation routine or an anxiety pill, I'd like to guide you through an exercise that will help you turn down the volume on the crazy. Because we're all a little crazy, right? Especially when it comes to work. Maybe it takes a certain level of insanity to start a business in the first place. Or perhaps an unnatural tendency to actually embrace risk.

Regardless of the qualities that got you to where you are today, I've noticed a common thread in my years of working with hundreds of different types of leaders and managers. The best ones don't necessarily behave the same way, have the same story, or follow the same path, but they do have one important thing in common— they are self-aware. That may mean awareness of delusion and egotism or humility and grace or anything in between.

Self-awareness is the first step towards bringing your life and your business to the next level: Knowing who you are and, perhaps more importantly, what you're best at. I need you to get there yourself if you're going to have a successful relationship with a virtual assistant, a project management tool, or anyone (and anything) else in your life, for that matter.

Becoming aware of what my mind and body needed to be healthy was the first turning point for me and my business. After that, determining what I loved to do, or at least what I liked to do, was the way to creating a sustainable career.

Here's how to get started.

Step 1: Audit Your Life

I have a sneaking suspicion that 90 percent of working adults don't actually know exactly what they do each day[1]. And I've experienced this first-hand. That feeling when you get to the end of a long work day and you're like, "Aw shoot, I worked really hard today! I'm so awesome!" But then you're also like, "Wait, what the hell did I just do all day?"

For most of us, work is responding to "urgent" emails, sitting in meetings, and crossing off as many tasks as possible so we can get to Friday happy hour faster.

But if you're sitting there thinking to yourself, "I feel like I'm spinning my wheels. I'm not really getting anything important done. I'm barely getting to the things I need to get done, let alone the things I want to

---

1. I don't have any data around this. It's just a hunch.

get done. I'm working all the time and I'm running my life into the ground," that's when it's time for an audit.

Here's how it works:

Grab a notebook and a pencil or pen. Pick a day to start. Usually, Mondays are a good bet because you're coming fresh off a weekend break. (Ha, you entrepreneurs are like, "I DON'T GET A WEEKEND BREAK, JESS, COME ON." I know. Bear with me. Try the Monday thing.)

At the top of each of five pages in your notebook, write the date. Then, list the hours, one per line, leaving a space between each hour, starting with the hour when you start work. I recognize that some of us start at 6 a.m. and others start at 10 a.m., or even 10 p.m! It doesn't matter when you start, but you'll generally have at least eight hours listed on each page.

Next, set a timer on your phone to go off every hour and get to work.

At the end of the first hour, write down everything you did, in detail.

It might look something like this:

- Reviewed last week's deliverables and made comments.
- Delivered comments in project management tool.
- Checked Facebook. Commented on three posts. Liked four posts.
- Checked email. Unsubscribed from some newsletters.

- Reviewed to-do list for the day. Crossed off "review last week's deliverables."
- Scheduled a meeting with two project leads to discuss progress.
- Checked Twitter. Followed a few more interior decorating blog accounts.
- Wrote an email to my boss telling her I need a raise. Oh wait. I'm the boss. I don't get a raise. At least not today.

Do this every hour. I'm serious. And don't depress yourself by thinking about it or looking back as you do it. Just DO it. Do it again tomorrow. And the next day. And the day after that. When you get to the end of the week, then you can take stock.

- How many hours did you spend in meetings? (You can also use your calendar for this, assuming you keep it up to date.)
- How many hours did you spend doing administrative work?
- How many hours did you spend doing someone else's job?
- How many hours did you spend doing something you hate?
- How many hours did you spend checking social media?
- How many hours did you spend doing something you love?
- How many hours did you spend doing something completely unnecessary?

I recognize that each week is different and if your schedule is truly all over the place, you may want to do this for several weeks, especially if your work involves any sort of travel because you want to evaluate your time on trips as well. However long you think you need to get a true average of where you're spending your time, do the painstaking work of jotting it all down.

This is the first step of becoming more self-aware.

Step 2: Hearts, Xs, Pluses, and Minuses

Now you know what you've been doing. It's time to figure out what you should and want to be doing.

Open up to a new page in your notebook and turn it to landscape mode. (Can you tell I use computers too much?) List the following categories at the top:

Love | Hate | Necessary | Useless

These are strong words, I know. But when you're forced to categorize each thing into one of these buckets, you'll start to get a clearer picture of what's in your way. Remember, you wouldn't be here if you didn't have a problem you were trying to solve.

I've done this exercise many times before and I decided to do it again for the sake of this book.

Here's a snippet of what my audit looked like. Oh, and by the way, my sweet puppy's name is Hummus in case you were wondering what "Hummus walk" could possibly mean.

MONDAY

9 AM: emails
9:30 AM: Review blog content for the week
10 AM: Metrics review / add to spreadsheet
10:15 AM: Schedule bank transfers
10:30 AM: Review guest posts
11 AM: Weekly editorial meeting
11:45 AM: Record monthly showrunners update
12 PM: Hummus walk
1 PM: Weekly team roundup
2 PM: reply to new biz inquiries
2:15 PM: Review podcast options + posts
2:30 PM: writing + editing
4 PM: check emails / FB group posts
4:30 PM: review Tuesday calendar
4:45 PM: edit case study
5:15 PM: wrap

TUESDAY

8:30AM: Emails
9AM: double check blog scheduling
9:15AM: leave for spin class
9:30AM: spin class
10:30AM: Hummus walk
11AM: emails
11:30AM: dentist
12PM: sprint meeting
1PM: new biz calls
2PM: contract creation for upcoming events
2:30PM: weekly call with Ann
3PM: calendar + email updates for Ann
3:38PM: review DPM social media calendar
4PM: weekly meeting with new client
4:30PM: review new proposals + approve
5PM: emails + review tomorrow calendar
6PM: wrap

WEDNESDAY

8:30AM: yoga
9:30AM: Hummus walk
10:30AM: emails
11AM: review + approve podcasts + posts
11:30AM: standup
12PM: Facebook, Twitter, Instagram
12:15PM: write special email for sponsor
12:30PM: Send email for review/check email
1PM: new biz calls
1:30PM: empty dishwasher, make food
2PM: book editing time
3PM: book marketing meeting
4PM: podcast scheduling + followups
4:30PM: emails, review blog posts + schedule
5PM: send test email for sponsor
5:15PM: book NYC + Raleigh flights
5:30PM: send invoices for NYC + Raleigh
6PM: wrap

THURSDAY

7:30AM: Spin class
8:30AM: Emails + schedule blog posts
9AM: Hummus walk
9:45AM: review proposals
10AM: research stats for book holes
11AM: new biz meetings
↓
1PM: check FB, Twitter, Instagram
1:15PM: writing + editing time
2:30PM: new biz meeting
3PM: emails, invoices, reviews on podcasts
3:30PM: check Traveling Mailbox + scan
4PM: check workers comp + disability
4:15PM: editing, creating graphics
4:45PM: guest post submissions
5PM: wrap

FRIDAY

9AM: emails
9:30AM: dog park
10:15AM: review next week's blog schedule
10:30AM: respond to new biz inquiries
10:45AM: create video for newsletter update
11AM: submit to 5 new speaking engagements
11:30AM: review duplicate content
12:30PM: duplicate content meeting
1:30PM: editing + writing time
3PM: calendar review
3:30PM: create JB newsletter for review
4PM: wrap + groceries!

Next, I went through and categorized my lists. I used four different color highlighters and assigned a color to each category. Hearts were pink. Xs were blue. Pluses were green. Minuses were yellow.

Hearts are for the things that I dream about doing. The things that I wake up excited for. For me, these are the easiest things to categorize first and I recommend you do the same.

The Xs are the things I deplore. Checking the dreaded Traveling Mailbox, which only ever houses letters from the government. Responding to unsolicited emails (I'm too nice sometimes). Pulling a report from Twitter or wherever. Paying taxes.

Don't cross out something so aggressively that you can't see what it says. The point is to be able to list these things later, so you've got to be able to see what they are! (But you can draw devil horns on them if you'll feel better. I'm not here to tell you how to live your best doodle-life!)

Pluses are for things that I might not love to do, but they're necessary for me to run my business. And more likely than not, they're things that only I can do.

Minuses are for things that are truly a waste of time. Checking social media if it's not directly related to a marketing project. Joining meetings that didn't really need me. Reviewing work that shouldn't have needed a review.

And of course, *doing* work that I should have delegated long ago. But you know, I'm not perfect either. Not yet... (Insert diabolical laughter here.)

Once you've placed your marks next to each activity, you're ready to put them into the categories you made on your landscape-oriented page. List each activity only once, even if you checked Facebook five times a day, eight days a week.

You may start to see patterns. For example, "meet with internal graphic design team" may go under your Heart column because your graphic design team is hilarious and great at holding productive meetings, but "meet with entire team every single day for another one of those miserable stand-ups" may go under your Minus category because these meetings simply aren't useful for you.

Also, as you're categorizing all the things, remember to think about each in terms of its highest relation to your actual job. You may LOVE checking Twitter, but is it necessary for you to be successful in your profession? For some industries, it certainly is. Think about PR and news professionals who need to know what's trending at any given moment. If you love checking Twitter and this is your job, you're in luck. All the hearts!

If checking Twitter incessantly isn't part of your job, it probably goes into the Minus category. Sorry. Life is hard sometimes.

(unnecessary things)

(things only you can do)

(things you hate doing)

(things you look forward to doing)

Don't Panic

MANAGEMENT

After you've placed every task from your week into its appropriate category, you should have a beautiful four-column sheet that looks something like this:

♥
- exercising
- internal team meetings/standups
- recording videos for newsletters
- writing
- submitting to speak at events
- new business meetings
- booking flights
- weekly meetings with clients
- planning events
- walking the dog

✗
- scheduling bank transfers
- checking the traveling mailbox
- going to the dentist
- creating contracts
- sending invoices
- scheduling podcasts
- nagging people
- writing sponsored content
- having useless meetings
- sending money to the government

✚
- checking email
- reviewing books
- reviewing podcasts
- replying to new business inquiries
- reviewing proposals
- reviewing business documents

▬
- checking email too frequently
- checking social media
- checking shopping sites for deals
- cleaning the house when I should be working

This is a very personal process, and wow, I just realized how much I just revealed to you by sharing my chart. These days, it looks like my love list is much longer than it used to be. That's good news! But there are also still a lot of Hates on the list, which is something to work on.

Remember, each job description is unique, each person's priorities are unique, and all the things that you love and hate are yours.

Step 3: Reflect (and Cry)

Now, if you're like most people, this is a depressing moment for you. Your Heart column likely holds your shortest list. Your Minus column is ridiculously full. And everything in between is just a sad, sorry combination of what's left: a mixture of Hate and Necessary.

Nobody wants to live like that. But the first step in making a change is to admit you have a problem, right? That's why we need to take a few moments to review what we are really doing here, day in and day out. We might laugh about it, we might cry about it, but ultimately we need to internalize what it means about who we are.

Are you happy about the way you're spending your days? If not, why not?

Are there things you can do to change? If not, why not?

A lot of us, myself included, have things in their lives that we do not have control over. Maybe our boss requires those stand-up meetings every day, and despite every effort we've made to make a case against them, we won't win that battle.

Okay, yeah, that's rough, but it's one of those things you're going to, unfortunately, have to move on from.

What I want you to reflect on are the things you CAN change. You don't have to figure out how to change these things yet. That comes later. Just look at those little balls of annoyance, grief, or frustration staring at you from the page. Think about *why* they're not making you happy, adding to your life, or boosting your career in some way.

Once you can understand what all those things are and the emotion behind them, you can start to become more aware of what drives you to be happy and productive.

Step 4: Create Your Blue Sky Scenario

I assume you've had a sufficient time to wallow in your sorrows at this point. There's nothing wrong with wallowing as long as you know when to quit it. Now, it's time to move into action.

This is when I take my handwritten list of Love, Hate, Plus, and Minus and move it into a digital format. Transfer your list into Evernote, Excel, Word, or wherever you feel most comfortable working in a table. Get everything transcribed into your tool of choice. This way, it will be easier for you to move information around. If you'd rather stay analog, that's totally fine. Just draw a line below your current list or start a new page with the same categories. I want you to have enough room to work.

😍	🙂	😐	⚠️
exercising	scheduling bank transfers	checking email	checking email too frequently
internal team meetings and standups	checking the Traveling Mailbox	reviewing blogs	checking social media
recording videos for newsletters and sending team updates	going to the dentist	reviewing podcasts	checking shopping sites for deals
writing	creating contracts	replying to new business inquiries	cleaning the house when I should be working...
submitting to speak at events	sending invoices	reviewing proposals	
new business meetings	scheduling podcasts	reviewing business documents	
booking flights	nagging people		
weekly meetings with clients	writing sponsored content		
planning events	having useless meetings		
walking the puppy	sending money to the government		

Now, imagine if you had no restrictions, financially or otherwise. It's sunny every day. The weather is a balmy 72 degrees and humidity is 0 percent. You get to design the way your week goes. The way your month goes. The way your *life* goes.

How does it look? What's your "blue sky" scenario?

Grab a glass of wine. Turn on your favorite Spotify playlist. Try to move to a mental place free of fear and judgment. I encourage you to really get creative here and start with the first column: Love.

Think about everything in your life, including things that are outside of your job. What is it that you truly love?

Is it spending time with your family? Is it spending time away from your family? (I won't tell.) Is it leading your team in bonding exercises? Traveling to speak to audiences of thousands? Quietly cracking the code of that software program you've been trying to build on and off for five years?

The reason I want you to start with what you love is not because I believe your entire life has to (or ever will) be made up solely of things you enjoy. As The Rolling Stones say, "You can't always get what you want." But they also say, "If you try sometimes, you'll find you get what you need."

Getting you to a point where at least 80 percent of the things you do every day don't make you want to bang your head against a wall is my goal here. Because banging your head against a way isn't good for that brain of yours. This way, you're getting what you need out of your life so you won't be a miserable schmuck who slogs around making other people miserable.

See? Fewer miserable schmucks = more happiness. You're making the world a better place, one Excel table at a time.

Once you've listed all the things that you love, things that make you happy, and things that you want more of in your life, it's time to move to the next critical step: Delegation.

Step 5: Get It Off Your Plate

According to a recent study by the Proceedings of the National Academy of Sciences of the United States of America, buying time promotes happiness[1]. And people who spent money to buy themselves time, particularly by outsourcing disliked tasks like cleaning and cooking, "reported greater overall satisfaction."[2]

Did you hear that? Greater overall satisfaction! Less stress! When you buy time, you buy happiness! Who knew it was that easy?

---

1. Whillansa, Ashley V., Elizabeth W. Dunnb, Paul Smeetsc, Rene Bekkersd, and Michael I. Nortona. "Buying time promotes happiness." PNAS, 13 June 2017, www.pnas.org/content/114/32/8523.full

2. Chokshi, Niraj. "Want to Be Happy? Buy More Takeout and Hire a Maid, Study Suggests." The New York Times, 27 July 2017, www.nytimes.com/2017/07/27/science/study-happy-save-money-time.html?_r=0.

(It's not, of course, but that's not the point of this part of the exercise. Just wait for it.)

During this process, I like to use a highlighting tool if I'm doing it digitally. An analog highlighter or multicolored pen situation works great if you're working on a piece of paper. Talk to me about color-coding anytime. I just love it!

Take a good hard look at your Hate list first. These are probably the things you want most to get off your plate, so they'll be easier to delegate. Highlight or draw a red circle around everything you think you can give to another team member, a boss, a client, or an assistant. (Don't lose your mind if you don't HAVE an assistant or another team member yet. It's okay. We are still in blue sky land where everything is possible, including work being done magically by an invisible wizard.)

If you have a few things left that you hate but that you know you can't delegate to someone else (yet), that's okay. Just leave them there and move on.

Repeat this process with your Plus list and your Minus list. Hopefully, you have a lot of highlights here by the end! If not, you may want to pick up a book or two about making a career change.

Now, it's time for the fun part. Create a brand new list with two columns:

1. For Me To Do | 2. For Someone Else To Do

Start copying everything over from your Love list, plus whatever is left from your Hate, Plus, and Minus lists onto the first column. Then, you guessed it, put everything else into the second column.

How does it look?

The results of this audit were pretty eye-opening for me the first time I went through the process. Granted, when I finally did stop to look at my life, it was obvious why I felt so sick and tired. Unfortunately, we often wait until something terrible happens before we take the time to reflect. For me, the bottom line was that I was holding on to so many responsibilities that I was not uniquely qualified to do. All of the things I felt like I "should" do were pushing out anything I actually wanted to do.

From this exercise, it turned out that in my perfect world, the things I loved and wanted to be doing were fewer than I realized. There were exactly six things:

1. Spread my knowledge through writing and speaking to help make my clients, team members, and colleagues better
2. Earn enough money to live a comfortable life
3. Travel to new places
4. Hear live music as much as possible
5. Eat and cook delicious food
6. Spend quality time with my significant other, family, and friends

Six things. Six things that I needed to keep in focus. Six things that would drive me to being the best possible version of myself. If anything else got in the way of those things, I needed to remember to evaluate whether they are truly necessary, and if they are, whether I need to do them myself or not.

One of the best pieces of advice I ever got was to figure out what mattered to me and make sure every decision I made would propel me toward that thing. I received that advice too young in my life and in my career to really understand what it meant. But I certainly get it now.

Of course, the stuff that matters and doesn't matter is not static. Jobs evolve. Lives change. I'm sure that if I decide to start a family one day, something like, "Make sure kids don't die" will become a pretty high-priority item for me.

Through this simple yet high-touch exercise, all of a sudden you can start to see everything that has been holding you back from living the life you want. It's all right there on the page staring at you in the face. All the things that have been bogging you down. All the things that have made you dread going to work. All the things that have kept you from the people you love. All the things that you thought you could never get away from.

They're looking up at you from that page in your notebook or on your laptop. They're saying, "Delegate meeeeee!"

And guess what? You can!

Now your eyes are open. Now you're aware of what you want to be doing and what you're best at doing. Let's get moving on getting rid of everything else.

chapter three

FIRST RELEGATE, THEN AUTOMATE

I know this is a book about virtual assistants, but I want to start this next section by saying this:

Not everything that you need to delegate should go to a person. There are plenty of tools, apps, and automated systems that you may not be utilizing to help you, so I'll share a few of those first. I believe that anything that can be automated by a bot or tool, should be. The human element of delegation should be saved for the most sensitive and important items on your list.

Step 1: Relegate!

To relegate is to get rid of, and if you get as much joy as I do from crossing things off a list, then you'll LOVE this tip.

Relegating is easy, and in fact, you've already started doing it. Your self-awareness exercise generated a list of things that are unnecessary for you or anyone to be doing—this is the Minus column. Get rid of them! Have you read the *Life Changing Magic of Tidying Up* by Marie Kondo? KonMari that shit! Girl, bye! If you're not going to help me, get out of my life! If you don't spark joy, say thank you and PEACE OUT!

That's it. See? You're making progress already.

Fine, fine, I know, this is easier said than done. So let's break down what it means for something to be unnecessary. Take a look at a project or task and ask yourself these questions:

1. **Why am I doing this?** This seems like an obvious question, but so many times in business we do things just because they've always been done and for no other reason. We never evaluate our workload so we never ask ourselves, "Why?" If your answer to this question is something along the lines of, "Because it's what my manager told me to do," or, "Because it's what I was trained to do," dig deeper. Ask the people around you, your bosses, or whoever it was that made you start doing that thing in the first place. If you can't find a good reason for doing something, it's probably not worth doing. Relegate.

2. **How is this contributing to my bottom line?** Now, hopefully you should never consider something "unnecessary" if it makes you money. That's why we're all here, right? Money, money, money! But there are lot of things that we do because we think

they're important, and we think they're driving business, but they're really not. I hate to tell you this, but some of the things on your Love list may be unnecessary things that you need to cut if they're not driving revenue or cutting costs. I'm sorry, but if you're spending time on things that aren't growing your profit margin, then you are actually doing the opposite. Time is money, remember? So, if checking your email 19 times in an hour doesn't drive new business, then stop it. Go create something. Or mentor a staff member. Or, I don't know, sleep. I believe in the positive ROI of sleep for making our brains sharp, money-making machines! Remove all of the things that aren't making you money now or in the future from your to-do list.

If you can't find a good answer for doing something and it's not contributing to your bottom line, stop doing the thing. Relegate it. Put it in a corner and tell it that its duty here is done. It's as simple as that.

The only reason an unnecessary task should stay on your plate is if it's something from which you find real joy. But I have to tell you, I think you should find other joys outside of unnecessary tasks, probably even outside of work, because you're not going to feel good crossing a bunch of worthless tasks off your list when they don't need to be there in the first place!

Step 2: Automate!

Some of the activities from your Hate, Necessary, and even Love columns will be recurring tasks. Maybe they're money-related, like paying bills or sending invoices. Perhaps they're weekly or monthly reports on some marketing activities. Or maybe an email reminder that needs to go out to every client on a certain day each month.

If you're comfortable with it, automating even one or two of these things could make a huge difference in your productivity levels. Tasks that take ten, five, or even two minutes add up quickly. Why not set them and forget them? Let the software and tools that exist out in the world work for you.

Let me give you an example. Let's say you need a report run every month on your social media activity. Ask yourself a few questions:

1. Am I using a social media management tool to manage my postings?
2. Does this tool provide any sort of analytics itself?
3. Can I get it to automatically email me a report every 30th of the month?

Even if you only answered "yes" to the first two questions, you've got a crap-ton of time saved because all a human being has to do is click "run" and "download" the report, as opposed to pulling out the data manually. Pro tip: I encourage you to become BFFs with your support tech people on the tools you use because sometimes they'll do you a favor and automate things for you.

Let me give you another example.

Let's say you have ten clients on a monthly retainer with you. The retainers may all be different, but bills always go out on the same day. A tool like Quickbooks Online or Freshbooks allows you to set up invoices to go out automatically on a recurring basis. Assuming you don't have any funny expenses or scope of work changes, this task gets done for you.

You can also set these tools up to send automatic reminder emails if someone doesn't pay in, say, 15 days, or whatever your terms are.

Here's one more example for the road.

If you're anything like me, you like to know what your clients are thinking about you. Not because you're egotistical, of course (heh), but because you want to make sure you're providing them with the quality of services they expect.

What if you had a simple, one-question survey that you sent all your clients at the end of every week?

There are a few ways to do this, but one of the easiest is setting all of your clients up on an email marketing platform like Mailchimp or ConvertKit (both free if you have a low enough number of subscribers on your list) or setting them all up as a group in Gmail (also free). You'll need to create a template for the email, but it can be short and sweet. Something like:

> *Hey, there, and HAPPY FRIDAY! It's the best day of the week again—lucky us!*

In an effort to make sure my services match up with your expectations, I'll be sending you a one-question survey every Friday. It's quick and easy for you, but it's important because it tells me how you're feeling about our work and gives you an opportunity to provide valuable feedback. Would you mind filling it out for me?

<insert survey link>

It's not a requirement of course, but I'd so appreciate it. And you can always respond directly to this email if you prefer to discuss more. Thanks for your time!

When Don't Panic does these, we actually attach them to our weekly email that we are already sending on Fridays, so it's not exactly automated. But we do use cute little graphics that we embed into the email and make it even easier for clients to tell us how they REALLY feel.

(We use a tool called GetFeedback for our surveys, by the way. Definitely recommended!)

After sending the initial "here's what I'm going to do" email (which isn't automated), you can create an automated email using Boomerang for Gmail or by creating a recurring email campaign in Mailchimp or ConvertKit. Every week at the time and day you designate, everyone on your client list (assuming you keep it up to date) will receive your survey.

Like magic!

I recommend analyzing every task you think you want to delegate for its automation potential so you can ensure you're not overlooking the amazing benefits that various online software tools have to offer.

Of course, if you need help figuring out what those benefits even are, you can always call me! I love working with tools that make my job easier.

Now, let's get to my favorite part: How to find a human being to help make your life approximately 9,178 times better.

Rule #2:

WHEN IN DOUBT, SOURCE IT OUT

chapter four

FACT: YOUR VIRTUAL ASSISTANT IS NOT A ROBOT

People think they're being pretty clever when they say things like, "Virtual assistant, eh? Are you even real or do you live up in the cloud?"

First of all, I beg of you, stop making that joke. It's not funny and it's a bit offensive to those of us who are making a living working virtually. I've said it a gajillion times and I'll say it again: virtual assistants are real people with real feelings, needs, and desires.

Now that we've gotten that out of the way, let's keep the magical process of the life audit rolling. After I finished my own life audit, relegated and automated the crap out of my task list, I was ready to begin delegating. It had become abundantly clear that I was not interested in performing any more work related to operations.

Creating proposals, contracts, and invoices were high on my Hate list. I didn't want to deal with the numbers. I needed a better online accounting system.

My next hire helped me organize my tangled web of files, get a better online accounting and contracts system in place, and ultimately, helped me see past the clutter and allowed me the time to plan the next phase of the business.

I thought back to the time before I started my own business. I could never shake the feeling that getting showered and dressed for work in the morning was a waste of time. (Still is. I'm sitting in my pajamas right now.) Getting in the car and driving to an office even more so. (TRAFFIC, right??) Efficiency was (and still is) my middle name and I was on a mission to bring that obsession with efficiency to other businesses.

With the newfound hours I suddenly had back in the day thanks to my operations manager, I began to look at my clients' lives from a holistic point of view.

What were they spending their time on? Were those things important? What was missing? What did they truly want?

That's when the true power of delegation came into focus. And I was more than happy to take all the things off their plate just so they could feel the same sense of relief I had begun to feel. A delicious sense of calm.

That would become my unique value proposition as I grew Don't Panic Management.

Just one problem: I learned that if a prospective client got it, they really got it. But if they didn't, they said things like, "Oh, you're a virtual assistant! Like that girl on my banking website that helps me know where to click!"

Well, not exactly, but I get why you think that!

Head, meet desk.

Here's another comment I've heard about virtual assistants: "I want to use a VA, but I have been burned in the past. ALL VIRTUAL ASSISTANTS ARE THE WORST!"

Obviously this is a gross exaggeration, but it makes sense. Until now, working with virtual assistants may conjure up visions of nightmare scenarios. In these worrisome visions, the angst often outweighs any potential relief.

- **Geographic concerns:** The client may not know where their VA lives, so they can't go to their house and look over their shoulder to make sure they're working.
- **Language concerns:** The client may have a different first language than the VA, so when they think they're asking for a very simple task, they receive a different result.
- **Communication concerns:** The VA may not be honest about what's going on in their life, so the client gets left high and dry without warning or explanation.
- **Security concerns:** There are plenty of stories of a VA who takes the money and runs. I just . . . I

can't explain this. Dishonesty is still rampant in the world, I guess.

- **Deadline concerns:** Organizational issues are common, but they're not the kinds of issues VAs should be running into.
- **Detail concerns:** Another common trait among humans is a lack of detail-orientation, but it's not one clients want from a VA.

We'll dig deeper into these concerns and more in the next chapter. Before we do, I want to be clear about a couple of things: I have nothing against virtual assistants in India, the Philippines, or any other country that isn't my own. I also don't have anything against people who are learning other languages, like English, to make a virtual career for themselves. I think that's pretty awesome, actually.

But virtual assistants definitely have a branding problem here. Too many individuals and companies have had bad experiences with virtual assistants, both domestic and international. Plus, Amazon's Alexa, Apple's Siri, and Microsoft's Cortana are coming to light as the "new" virtual assistants that are taking over the world.

I find myself constantly asking, "How am I going to explain what a virtual assistant agency is to potential clients or colleagues?" And, "Do I need to have a different explanation of what I do depending on who I'm talking to and their level of prior knowledge?"

To the latter question, I've learned that, unfortunately, the answer is yes. One elevator pitch does not fit all.

If you're not a savvy internet professional, I say something like, "I run a company that provides executive and marketing assistant services on a part-time, virtual basis."

If you work on the internet, I say things like, "I run a virtual assistant agency that focuses on helping entrepreneurs, executives, and managers get more work done through outsourcing all the things that bog them down."

And if you're an online pro who has actually used a virtual assistant before, I may go a bit deeper. "I run a personalized matchmaking service for clients to find the perfect virtual assistant. The goal is to develop a long-term relationship that will grow their business over time."

I'd love to get to the point where I could introduce my business that way every time. We're not there yet and we won't be for a while. But that's okay, because here's the most important thing: As frustrated as I get explaining the whole VA industry to people sometimes, I absolutely cannot get enough of seeing the look on people's faces when the light switch clicks and they start to get it. I mean *really* get it.

"Wait, so, I ended up in Vegas a week early last month because I screwed up the flight dates. You can book those correctly for me?"

"I HATE sending invoices every month. You can send those accurately for me?"

"I don't know how to get my PowerPoint deck from 4:3 ratio to 16:9. You can do that for me?"

"I hate negotiating speaking fees. I want to get what I'm worth. You can push back and get what I want for me?"

Okay, okay, and this one:

"Is there anything you DON'T do???"

Well, of course. VAs are not a bunch of genies. (I wish!)

Virtual assistants exist to provide one very specific solution:

To gracefully and reliably accomplish all the things that you can't do, hate doing, or shouldn't be doing in your business so that you can spend your time on big ideas.

So let's start this section by quelling the preconceived notions, myths, and misconceptions about virtual assistants so you can be crystal clear about their power (and lack thereof). Bonus points if you can help spread the knowledge to all your friends and family who are culprits in perpetuating the spread of these misconceptions. I promise hugs and high fives!

chapter five

10 COMMON MISCONCEPTIONS ABOUT VIRTUAL ASSISTANTS

The whole, "Are you a human being or are you a robot" question isn't the only one that virtual assistants have to overcome day in and day out. There are countless other myths and misconceptions about who virtual assistants are, what they can do, and how they can help. Here are the top ten.

1. Anyone Can Be a VA

Some people think that anyone who has a pulse and a laptop can become a virtual assistant. A college student with the curiosity and smarts to learn how to do the work via YouTube videos, for example. This is partially true. Look, I know that virtual assistant work isn't rocket science. Theoretically, anyone *could* do it. But not anyone can do it well, and that's the rub. It's not easy to find ideal clients, figure out what they need, set up rates and contracts, and then, of course, deliver great work on time.

Individuals who have the experience, the chops, and the interest in working with a VA agency have the luxury of working with a support team who can help with things like finding the right clients, setting up contracts, and handling deliverables. Personally, I think that's part of the reason why VAs who work at an agency actually *can* do their best work—they're not bogged down by the red tape and detailed administrative work that comes with running a business. But managing tasks for multiple clients and projects can get hairy, even with a strong project management tool. Plus, remembering who likes which report in what format, for example, can be a headache.

Virtual assistants have to be extremely organized, deadline-driven, detail-oriented, and be able to get into clients' heads about what they really need.

It's not an easy task. And it's half the reason why many VA relationships fail.

I've heard many prospective clients say, "I've got my sister-in-law working on it," or, "I found a college kid to help me for half the price." Okay, awesome, that sounds more cost effective in the short term. And if they're truly qualified, sweet! You've got the best of all worlds.

On the other hand, if you're spending all your time reviewing their work, prodding them about deadlines, and trying not to get pissed off as they ask you yet another question whose answer could have been found on Google, is paying less for a less-experienced, less-skilled assistant really saving you any money?

Now, I'm not saying you have to get a degree in virtual assistance to be a great VA. (Does that even exist? Should I start a school for VAs??) But you do need to have some administrative, customer service, and/or project management experience to succeed at the role.

You also have to, you know, want it. At least a little bit.

2. It's Impossible to Communicate Effectively With a VA

When you're not in the same room as another person, looking them in the eye, and witnessing their body language, it can be difficult to have a conversation. As a result, a virtual relationship requires more attention and focus on strong communication. That's part of the nature of virtual environments, but it doesn't mean that having great conversations, providing important directions, and getting to know your VA on a personal level isn't possible.

Perhaps this one is more of a personal issue than anything else because, look, some people just can't communicate effectively. Period. Whether it's on the phone, via email, or face-to-face. I'll tell you right now, if you're one of those people then you definitely should not work with a virtual assistant. I repeat: DO NOT WORK WITH A VA! At least not yet. You know, maybe going to some continuing education classes on effective communication could help. Or working with a coach. Seriously, communication is a huge part of life if you work or live with other people.

You need to have strong communication skills to be a manager of any kind, especially one that manages a person and/or team remotely. What does that mean?

- Giving clear instructions via email, phone, or video screen share.
- Providing clear deadlines at the start of a project using a project/calendar management tool.
- Offering feedback excessively, especially in the beginning, and giving more positive feedback than negative. (Read Kim Scott's *Radical Candor* if you need help with this, or listen to her accompanying podcast.)
- Listening to the questions and ideas of the team in order to understand how you can give them what they need to succeed.

If you can do these kinds of things in person, there's no reason you can't do them virtually. You'll just need different set of tools in your box in order to do so.

Phone, email, and Skype/Zoom are the most common virtual communication tools. Some less common ones are real-time social communication tools like Sococo, Facebook, and Slack. I know people who manage their entire workflows and communications solely through these tools (which is totally impressive, but also totally unnecessary).

We're becoming better and better at using those little devices in our pockets to communicate with friends and family. There's no reason we can't use them for professional purposes, too.

3. A VA's Degree (Or Lack Thereof) Is a Crucial Element to Their Success

The path to becoming a virtual assistant has been touted as an easy way for individuals with limited experience and expertise to make a living. As a result, there are many assistants being hired to do work they are not qualified for. That doesn't mean, however, that the organizational, tactical, and communication skills required to become a great VA are only taught in a college or continuing education environment.

Internships, restaurant jobs, caring for an ailing neighbor, earning a degree in an unrelated field, or managing a household are all excellent experiences that can help form the skills necessary to becoming an outstanding virtual assistant.

There's a stigma about the type of skills needed to be a VA. That it's sooooo easy to push numbers around and send files.

Sure. There are a lot of administrative tasks that are pretty mindless on their own. Click calendar time. Add appointment. Send invitation to guests. Cross off list.

But being a kickass VA requires more than checking the boxes.

Let's take it back to those *Mad Men* days. Remember their incredible secretaries? They ran shit! The men in the office almost literally could not function without them. While it's no longer about being a pretty lady in a tight skirt, it's still about having unbendable patience, impeccable organizational skills, and an iron fist when it comes to deadlines.

So, maybe becoming a VA doesn't require a college degree these days, but it certainly requires a level of intelligence, experience, and street smarts to be great at it. Those can all be acquired in a variety of ways.

Take me, for example. I went to one of the best business schools in the country and got a double major in Marketing and International Business, a concentration in Entertainment Media, and a minor in Russian.

A lot of my internships and work experiences required me to speak eloquently with people, organize meetings, files, events, people, you name it, and generally be all things to all people, including myself—running, skipping, walking, racing from 8 a.m. class to 9 a.m. internship to 3 p.m. restaurant job to 11 p.m. homework.

As much as I wanted to tell guests to GO AWAY, YOUR TABLE ISN'T READY YET at the restaurant I was hostessing at, or GO HERE, SIT DOWN, EAT THIS, BE QUIET to attendees at an event I was managing, I learned that you don't get anywhere in life with poor people skills. And that being busy is no excuse for being a jerk.

Ultimately, I learned that all of this life and work juggling back in college prepared me to become a virtual assistant, perhaps even more than my academic studies (but don't tell my parents that). The skills I learned in the real working world were paramount in building my communications, organizational, and customer experience skills, which are essential in the virtual assistant world, and I'd argue in the personal life world as well. Life issues parallel work issues and if you have the skills to solve one, you can solve the other. It's just a simple mindset shift.

Perhaps I didn't need the minor in Russian to become a great VA. But perhaps the combination of working hard to become proficient at a new language, strategize with classmates on big projects, and earn money on the side helped me manage the many professional responsibilities I have today.

Don't ever let someone's degree or lack thereof dissuade you from considering them for the job. Skills can be taught. Life experiences, aligning values, and a drive to succeed cannot.

4. I Can Only Afford an International VA

Let's really break this one down.

International VAs (specifically in countries like India and the Philippines) are generally more affordable than US-based VAs because their cost of living is lower.

Chris Ducker, founder of Virtual Staff Finder and Youpreneur, has a ton of experience working with

Filipino VAs. I asked him to share some of his thoughts on when and why to use a Filipino VA in particular.

I started Virtual Staff Finder in 2008 to bridge an outsourcing gap between international entrepreneurs and experienced VAs in the Philippines. Virtual assistants in the Philippines are usually the first port of call for most entrepreneurs delving into the VA world for the first time. They are smart, speak great English, and have solid experience in the industry. Their lower cost bracket makes them desirable to first time virtual hirers, so the market has flourished in the Philippines over the last decade and shows no sign of slowing down anytime soon.

The people that work best with Filipino VAs are online entrepreneurs that have repetitive tasks that need to be handled in a professional, timely fashion. If you expect your Filipino VA to run your business, think again! These brilliant employees are doers, not business partners. They'll help you by supporting your business growth, but YOU will need to be the one making the plans and executing them!

Becoming a VA is a common and desirable career choice in countries like the Philippines, so there is a large hiring pool for you to work with. If you can find the right one, they'll have the same skills as a US-based VA and potentially be just as reliable even though they're in another time zone.

What you need to remember about hiring internationally is that it may require more time and energy on your end because you'll need to more deeply vet the assistant, check their references, and do a lot more training to overcome any cultural differences, language barriers, or mismanaged expectations. Unless it's another country that shares the same language as you, you'll have to address the language barrier head-on because it often prevents the assistant from doing any public-facing work and writing for you. So don't pigeonhole yourself if you need more than simple data-entry or reporting tasks.

Virtual assistants come in all shapes, sizes, and prices, so I recommend that you look inside the country you live, at least to start. You may not find them for $1 per hour, but for $10 per hour? Maybe!

And remember that time is money. So you can't simply base your costs on how many dollars per hour you're paying the assistant—you have to think about your own hourly rate and how many dollars per hour of your own time you're using to find, hire, train, and nurture the right person.

Certainly look for what you can afford, but don't think that just because you're a small operation, or even a solopreneur, that you can't afford someone within your own geographical borders.

5. VAs Are Working As a Means to an End

At Don't Panic, we've had mothers, fathers, nonprofit leaders, artists, missionaries, actors, freelance writers, gardeners, chefs, and everything in between come to us looking for work. Are they passionate about the other things they do? No doubt! But are they trying to get VA work solely because they need money to support the other thing?

Not always.

You see, virtual assistant work can be extremely fulfilling for people who know they have the education, experience, and training to make someone else's life better. And people's lives don't get better merely from data entry. Okay, maybe some people's lives do. I shouldn't judge.

The litmus test for me is always this: If I wasn't getting paid, would I still do this?

For many working professionals, the answer would be no. Because many people would rather take naps every day, spend time tending to their gardens, visit with friends, go on a road trip to visit every theme park in the country, or do whatever else it is that they're passionate about.

On the contrary, a lot of people who become VAs do so because simply living their passion isn't enough. As soon as you live your passion full-time there's the risk it will no longer BE your passion.

Variety is the spice of life. The best (and happiest) VAs I've worked with are those who spend part of their time doing the thing they love, such as raising children, painting, or baking bread, and the other part of their time drafting checklists, writing blog posts, researching the next big trend in cloud computing, and seeking the best flight (with the cheapest upgrade) from Atlanta to Amsterdam.

These VAs are multi-talented and are fulfilled by utilizing all of their skills in different ways—not just the ones they studied, or are most fun, or bring in the most cash.

6. VAs Already Know How to Do Exactly What I Want

Maybe I've convinced you that really great VAs are like magical, mystical beings that climb out of the computer and into the deepest corners of your brain. They cleverly pull out the why, the when, and the how of your business. They give you the mental space and time to do only the things you are uniquely qualified to do and nothing else. And they do it automatically without any training needed.

Yeah, I may have dug myself into a hole with that one. Sorry about that.

VAs are supposed to have skills and they're supposed to have experience with other clients that can help inform them on the best and worst ways of getting things done.

But you, my dear, are special. Your business is unlike any other. Your set of tools, outcomes, and processes are different than the rest and even if you're not particular about them, you still need to remember to share that information with your VA. This is a good thing! It's important to differentiate yourself from everyone else.

For these reasons, you can't assume your VA will know how you like things to be done. You know what they say about assumptions . . .

You may be able to avoid any mismanaged expectations from the start by providing a clear job description and list of sample tasks. Also, a test project and evaluation before they begin work will help you determine if this particular person has some of the skills you want and is able to follow a procedure that's similar to your own.

Always remember you will need to do some work getting your assistant up to speed. That no matter how great they are, they can't read your mind. At least not yet. So you have to tell them what you want and be extra clear about it.

7. A VA Can't Do the Same Things as an EA

This one is partly true, and I'll share a few ways to determine whether you need a VA (virtual assistant) or an EA (executive assistant) in a following section. For example, unlike an EA who works full-time in your office, a VA can't go to Starbucks and deliver that half-caff-soy-latte-with-extra-foam to your desk.

(But they CAN use Postmates to have someone else retrieve and deliver it! Technology for the win!)

Other than specific in-person tasks, however, VAs can do just about everything virtually that an in-office executive assistant can do. So, you know, lucky for you!

This is part of the reason virtual work has become so powerful. When we can work from the comforts of our own home, couch, porch, wherever, why would we want to be beholden to an office surrounded by people bothering us for things all day?

I know, I'm biased. I have been working from home since 2010. I get so much more done when I'm alone in my house with my music and my puppy and my snacks. I get that this environment doesn't work for everyone.

But when you consider the cost of an office space, desks, chairs, coffee makers, couches, more snacks, keeping the kegerator full, and buying toilet paper, working virtually seems like a good alternative, provided you're not building car engines or something more physically hands-on.

So, while you should always remember to do what makes the most sense for your situation, don't ever think that just because you've "always done it this way" that it's the only way, or more importantly, that it's the right way for your business. If you don't have a full-time job for an EA and you don't need that level of in-person support, a VA is a great option. It's a whole new world out there and sometimes change is good.

8. VAs Can Do Work at the Same Level As a Specialist

It pains me a little bit to write this one down, but it's true: VAs are not always as skilled as specialists. For example, if you're paying a VA $50 or $60 per hour to edit your podcast recordings, you can't expect the same level of quality as if you paid an audio engineer $150 or $300 per hour.

This goes back to the whole "you get what you pay for" conversation. If you want professional engineer-level sound quality for your podcast, you should consult with a professional sound engineer. They can help you get the equipment you need to sound amazing and can help you produce a recording that tickles the ear drums.

If, on the other hand, you're just starting out with a new podcast that is about anything other than, well, audio engineering quite frankly, then the skills that a virtual assistant has to piece it together using free or inexpensive software should be enough.

Because when you're starting something new, you don't necessarily WANT to pay top dollar right off the bat. If a free tool like Audacity includes the audio editing elements you need, why pay hundreds of dollars for an advanced piece of software like Pro Tools? You want to release your minimum viable product, the thing that gets you out there—and yes, sounds decent—but won't break the bank.

At least until you're earning so much money from sponsorships, new speaking gigs, and a book deal from your podcast. Then, have at it! Splurge on the best damn podcast producer out there. Or at that point, realize that if you got there using a VA's skills, you might be just fine keeping things where they are (and maybe giving your VA a little raise!).

9. VAs Are Available 24/7

So, I'm paying for 20 hours of VA support per week. I can use these hours whenever I want. If I'm working late, my VA works late. If I work on the weekends, my VA does, too. Isn't that how it works?

Oh, my dear friend! You know I love you. And I'll tell you this: MAYBE it works that way. For some people. This could be part of your expectation-setting process that you go through when you are interviewing and onboarding your VA.

Never forget that VAs are 1099 contractors, not W2 employees (at least in the majority of situations). Unless you are hiring employees, you cannot dictate which hours they work or how they get their work done (on the couch vs. at a desk vs. balancing their laptop on top of their cat). This is something you may want to consult with a labor lawyer about so you understand the distinction more clearly.

Some VAs will provide stipulations for emergency work or "on-call" support. They may charge double for this and may require advance notice. That's within their right.

The only situations in which asking for on-call support is reasonable are:

1. **You've got a big launch and there are lots of on-the-fly tasks that need to get done in a short period of time.** Oftentimes with launches, there's a product associated and so you need on-call customer

support while the first orders come through. You need your assistant to monitor the inbox for the first 24-48 hours, making sure nothing blows up. You'll need to discuss this with your assistant and make a plan in advance because only a robot can stay awake answering customer service emails for 48 hours straight and—I don't know how many times I have to say it—your assistant is not a robot. At least as far as I know.

2. **You have a major personal illness or family emergency that prevents you from working or handling as much as you normally would.** Now, normally these things cannot be predicted, so unfortunately you may not be able to give your assistant notice. If you've developed a close-knit relationship with your assistant, however, and they don't have any of their own emergencies to deal with, you may be able to convince them to work extra for you. You may also ask them to tag in a fellow virtual assistant or find another short-term one to bear some of the brunt of the extra workload. If you're working with a virtual assistant agency, they'll most likely be able to provide the extra support you need within your existing contract with them. Of course, you'll need to pay everyone for their time, and that may not be feasible for you, so try to be rational and reasonable about what, at the bare minimum, must get done while you're out. If it is a true emergency, clients, customers, and colleagues will understand. At least they should. If they don't they're assholes and you should throw them all in the garbage.

10. VAs Don't Need to Be Treated Like Regular People

I can only imagine what goes through the heads of some of our most heartless clients when they wake up in the morning and decide to word-vomit all over their VA. I've seen the result of these thoughts upfront and personal and it looks something like this:

La la la, my VA is in another state/country and I've never met them in person nor will I ever so I can roid-rage all over their inbox because I woke up on the wrong side of the bed and belittling another person makes me feel better, la la la!

Oh, how I wish these folks would get a therapist. Or go to church. Or simply do whatever it takes to understand that everyone, regardless of job title, shape, skin color, religion, sexual orientation, gender, or anything else, should be treated equally and with respect.

The only people who get poor treatment are the ones in the video games. Because they captured your princess and you need to get her back.

Just because you can't see the moon all the time doesn't mean it's not there. Same with your VA. You may not hear from her every other second or feel her presence in the chair next to you, but she's there. And she's a living, breathing human with feelings and emotions.

Oh, and you know what else? She doesn't HAVE to work with you. She has the expertise and the communication skills to work with other clients besides you. It's easy to forget, I know. You may be the one helping her pay her bills, but you're also providing her livelihood. If you have a good one, your VA is worth her weight in gold, especially given the sheer amount of opportunities available to virtual assistants these days. So please, try to remember to treat her that way. Otherwise she'll end her contract with you to go work with someone who doesn't treat her like a pile of poop.

If you have concerns about something your VA has or hasn't done for you, you can certainly address them. I'm not saying you can never give constructive feedback to someone who is working with you. Just be sure to keep things professional, specific, and actionable. There is a way to be kind but firm. You don't need to be a jerk.

Now that you understand a little bit about what virtual assistants are for, let's do a little soul-searching to figure out whether a virtual or executive solution is right for you.

chapter six

PICK YOUR POISON: ANALOG OR DIGITAL?

We are living in a digital world, but I am still an analog girl. Madonna taught me that. Nothing can replace someone hand-writing your daily to-do list or printing out pages of an article for you to edit. This style of work isn't possible or, perhaps more importantly, desirable for everyone in today's economy. For many, it makes much more economic sense to hire remote workers and it often makes more business sense as well, especially if you're looking for a certain set of skills and experiences that may or may not exist in the small fishing village where you've been raising your family and growing your business.

Slowly but surely, the virtual assistant concept is beginning to reach the masses as a practical and affordable option for getting work done, but we're still not quite there yet. (Hence part of the reason for this book . . . duh.) I find myself over-explaining what Don't Panic Management does when sometimes it seems like the easiest explanation is, "We're an assistant service that works remotely."

Part of the challenge is that the word "assistant" itself conjures up ideas of running errands, getting coffee, and filing documents. Which is often true for an executive assistant (EA) and is extremely valuable. The EA was designed to be the right hand to the executive, preempting any questions with answers and coming to the rescue when called.

Cue images of Anne Hathaway awkwardly dragging clothing samples around hallways while Meryl Streep rolls her eyes.

But that's really not the role of a virtual assistant at all, and I'd like to clear up the difference once and for all.

Virtual assistants often have some very different skill sets than executive assistants. They may be terrible at ordering coffee and answering phones, but great at organizing files and creating beautiful-looking PowerPoint templates.

Still, virtual assistants are not for everyone.

Perhaps you need the availability of a full-time employee, or maybe you simply communicate better in person. Some business owners have come to us in search of a VA because they just can't find anyone local who's qualified to help them, but that doesn't necessarily mean a virtual solution will be the best fit either.

So, what's a talented business owner or manager like you to do? Should you pursue hiring a virtual assistant, or is an in-house executive assistant your best option?

You may already have an idea, or you may not have a clue. Either way, I've set out a list of five questions that you need to ask yourself and answer, very honestly, to get to the bottom of it. And if you end up choosing the EA route, I won't be offended. You just may have to give this book away to someone else who needs it!

1. Will I need any in-person support?

This is the first and biggest question you need to ask yourself, as it's an obvious make-or-break requirement. If your task list includes things like going to the bank, picking up the mail, and making copies, then an executive or personal assistant is going to be the best fit for you.

But if you're looking for things that can be done online from anywhere, a virtual assistant should be able to fit the bill.

Some common virtual assistant tasks include scheduling meetings (both online and in-person), booking travel, researching content for writing projects, sending invoices, tracking expenses, and creating and/or formatting documents. A more advanced assistant can also help with more involved bookkeeping, implementing marketing activities, researching and booking speaking engagements, media/content production, and lots more.

2. What's my preferred communication style?

Is looking someone in the eye important to you? Do you want to be able to track your assistant's every move? Or are you just as comfortable getting email updates and having a weekly phone or video call?

Everyone communicates differently and values different aspects of their communication channels with staff. Depending on the nature of your business, you may be perfectly comfortable communicating exclusively via email and chat (or maybe a text message or call here and there).

But there are many businesses and structures that do best with in-person communications, especially if the nature of your business involves more sensitive communications or very timely projects.

Consider how you like to communicate to someone and how you prefer to be communicated with. Both are important in determining whether a virtual or executive assistant is right for you.

3. Is it my way or the highway?

There's nothing wrong with wanting things done a certain way. However, it's much easier to train and monitor work processes when you have someone sitting right next you. If this is how you prefer to run your company, an EA is probably the better fit for you.

If you're more concerned with the outcome than the process, a virtual assistant is a great solution because they often have experiences from other clients or projects that they can implement to get things done quickly and successfully for you.

4. How timely are my projects?

Do you expect an email to be answered within 15 minutes? An hour? Same day? Are projects expected to be done within one business day?

It's important to evaluate the urgency of your tasks and projects in order to determine expectations of timeliness. If you expect someone to do something the second they are handed the task, you may want to do just that: physically hand them a task. If you're more of a long-term planner than a last-minute taskmaster, you can count on a virtual assistant to complete their tasks within your specified reasonable time frame.

5. How do I feel about assistant-sharing?

When you hire a virtual assistant, there's a good chance they are working in a part-time contractor capacity. This means they are likely to have other clients, which is an important marker for the government to see so you don't get in trouble for hiring someone as a contractor when they should have actually been an employee. Oftentimes the other clients your virtual assistant works with are using them for the same purpose that you would use them for.

Are you okay with that?

If the answer is no, you may be better off having someone in-house and as more of an employee status (part-time or full-time) as opposed to a contractor. That gives you more control over their schedule as well as the projects they can and cannot take.

If you're sitting here thinking, "Hey, that's awesome! I'd love to have someone who has the experience of working with others so we can all share ideas and best practices," then the VA relationship will be no problem for you.

A Combination Approach

If you know you want a virtual assistant but also have some analog needs to take care of, there are a few solutions for you. One way to get the benefits of a more qualified and trained assistant while also getting your in-person errands done is to hire a part-time virtual assistant and a part-time executive assistant or intern. You can clearly delineate the tasks that each should do and keep the two roles completely separate. It's more effort to manage in terms of personnel, of course, but it can be a great solution for the people who need a hands-on solution but are having trouble finding someone local.

You can also try using a service like Task Rabbit to take care of your one-off errands or in-house projects. They're an affordable solution that exists in most major cities.

Ultimately, I believe the choice comes down to control and how much of it you want to have. So remember, as you're answering these questions, don't think about what you *should* do or how you *should* operate. You need to be extremely honest with yourself about your needs. It's okay to want things done quickly. It's okay to be a micromanager. What's important is knowing yourself and your business, being extremely aware of your needs, and being realistic about your expectations so that you can find the right person to fit the role. (Go back to your life audit here if you need to; it's there for you to use as an ongoing resource!)

chapter seven

KNOW YOUR OPTIONS: THE FREELANCER, AGENCY, VA, HYBRID DECISION

I wish I could say that a virtual assistant could solve every need, from gathering your morning latte to leading your sales and marketing strategy, but it's just not the case. Depending on your resources and what you're trying to achieve, there are several different options for you to choose from. I'll offer some insight into who can do what, where, when, and why.

The Freelancer

The Situation: You've got a big project that needs to be managed from start to finish. It has a lot of moving parts, from web design and development to marketing and promotion. You don't do these projects often, so you don't have a department in-house to cover them.

The Solution: This may be a job fit for a freelancer or two who have some higher level experience and can own the project from start to finish.

Freelancers are generally very specialized at certain things and they like to take projects that fit within the scope of their specialty. You'll often see graphic design freelancers, web development freelancers, and freelance writers because all of these specialties take a bit more experience and expertise than, say, travel-booking. (Although I won't knock the fine art of finding that perfect flight with upgraded seats for a fair price.)

The Specs: Freelancers usually thrive on serving a small number of clients at a time. After all, they only have so many hours in a day! As a result, some of the best freelancers might be booked weeks or months out, so you'll have to consider the urgency of your project and whether you're willing to wait for a particular person to be available.

You can find freelancers on aggregated marketplaces like Upwork.com and Behance.net as well as by chatting with people in your network. Another great way to find freelancers is to do a LinkedIn search with "<project name> freelancer". So, graphic design freelancer, marketing strategy freelancer, video production freelancer, etc.

If you use a marketplace or LinkedIn, you'll be able to analyze their experiences and see previous projects they've worked on. Ideally, you'll also be able to find their professional website so you can dig deeper into their work and start to gather some details about their style and approach.

My favorite way to find really good freelancers is definitely through searching on LinkedIn. The great thing about LinkedIn is that you can see which search results are connected to people you already know. That adds a layer of credibility to their profiles and allows you to ask your connections for a recommendation, good or bad.

And duh, Google works, too. You just might get a ridiculous amount of results, many of which will be bogus.

The Cost: Freelancers generally charge either by the hour or by the project. Oftentimes, their project rates are developed using an hourly rate times estimated number of hours, and that hourly rate ranges pretty widely depending upon their number of years of experience and their perceived expertise.

I've worked with freelancers who charge anywhere from $25 per hour to $500 per hour.

Therefore, you'll need to be clear about your budget and the level of quality you're expecting because you can really pay anything for any project.

Rely heavily on testimonials and recommendations, especially because freelancers are notorious for "ghosting" (disappearing without a trace mid-projects), just as some virtual assistants are. You want to make sure you find someone who not only can do the work you're asking for, but who has strong communication and project management skills.

Freelancers will often be open to negotiating rates and timelines if they feel they can be successful with your project. Also, if you can promise them future work, they may want to offer you a lower rate in an attempt to ensure the repeat-business.

The Agency

The Situation: You have a new initiative that you've been dragging your feet on for months, partly because you don't know where to start and partly because you know you don't have the resources to implement the new idea.

Many times, these situations arise from a boss, a book, or a hunch, and they need to happen over the course of a few weeks or months. They are not one-and-done projects—they're usually the sort of things that will need ongoing maintenance post-launch.

The Solution: The agency model is designed to provide everything from strategy to implementation under one roof, all managed by someone that's not you. This is awesome because ideally all you'll need to do is provide your vision, your goals, and your budget, and they'll take them off your hands to find a solution. You won't need to worry about dealing with the writer, the artist, the producer, or whoever else is on the team. You'll communicate with one account manager who will herd all the cats for you.

The Specs: Agencies usually work with really big companies on really big projects. They become partners to companies that don't have the bandwidth, or frankly, the desire to do it all.

This is why you'll often see a telecom company that has five different agencies on retainer. They want to focus on their technology, sales, and customer service, but they don't want to worry about PR, marketing, or legal (just to name a few).

The Cost: Higher-level agencies are expensive, but that's because they are meant to be a one-stop-shop. They are also designed to become a partner in your business. If you're trusting an agency to see a large project or initiative through from start to finish, you don't want to worry about whether or not they'll deliver. With agencies, you're paying for top-notch work that includes all the project management and nitty-gritty admin that inevitably comes with working on big projects.

The VA

The Situation: Some would argue that a virtual assistant fits under the "freelancer" category. I agree, but only to a certain extent, which is why I listed it as its own category here.

Usually freelancers are more specialized than VAs are, and as we learned earlier, VAs are not always specialists. Freelancers tend to do one thing and one thing only. They aren't generally willing to jump into other scopes of work because they're getting paid well for the one thing that they want to be doing.

VAs, on the other hand, are more generalists. They may work on a certain type of work, but they're not beholden to one specific task or another. They are often fast learners and are eager to pick up new skills.

If you need ongoing or intermittent support on lower-level tasks, such as data entry, administrative work, marketing implementation (not strategy), research, or the like, that's where a VA may be your best bet.

The Solution: Unlike freelancers, most VAs prefer to have a small corral of clients that do not turn over. They like to have ongoing, consistent work and they like to develop relationships with their clients for the long haul.

The Specs: Hopefully now you know that VAs exist all over the world, have different sets of skills, and have different levels of experience. You can truly find a VA for anything you can think of, provided the things you need can be done on the internet. Generally, VAs are less expensive than freelancers or agencies, which explains their growing popularity.

Because VAs are typically not as specialized as freelancers, however, you'll need to make sure you're hiring for the skill as much as for the personality. Similar to the ways you'd find a freelancer, make sure you're using "marketing virtual assistant" or "podcasting virtual assistant" or "data entry virtual assistant" when you're making your search queries as opposed to merely "virtual assistant."

The Cost: VAs charge anywhere between $1 and $150 per hour, but in my experience the average rate for US- and Europe-based VAs is usually $15-$40 per hour for most administrative-level tasks. Going up from there, you'll see higher rates for more complex work that requires a higher level of knowledge or experience.

Many VAs scale their rates depending on the type of work they're doing. So, they may charge $20 per hour for schedule management but charge $50 per hour for copywriting. You will also find rate differences when you look at the experience levels of different VAs. Someone who has just graduated college may be closer to $10-$15 per hour while someone who has worked as a VA for ten years may be in the $40-$50 per hour range.

We'll talk more about how to find VAs as well as how to evaluate costs and experience in the next section, so hang tight!

The Hybrid

The Situation: Let's say you have several ongoing projects or daily/weekly tasks that keep the trains running on time in your business. Things are pretty steady, but you want to increase your bandwidth so you can tackle a few new initiatives.

The Solution: The Hybrid model is an agency of virtual assistants. I'm not talking about a marketplace like Upwork, Red Butler, or the like. I'm talking about an actual agency where there's accountability and backup support, similar to a web development agency, a public relations agency, or a marketing agency.

The goal is to get the skills and dedication of a virtual assistant but with the set systems, processes, and additional support of an agency. In many ways, it's the best of all worlds.

The Specs: I like to think I invented the hybrid model because it was what I wished I'd had as an entrepreneur. I didn't want to rely on one person, but I couldn't afford a big agency. I wanted to have the personalization factor of working with an individual and I wanted the agency team behind them. Because I am not quick to trust people. And I'm a control freak.

There was born, Don't Panic Management.

Don't Panic is the only hybrid I know of that operates exactly the way we do with personalized matchmaking and rigorous hiring and testing procedures, but there are plenty of other virtual assistant agencies out there. Each one has its own unique selling proposition. The best way to find them is to, as always, talk to your friends or do a Google search. You should always look at reviews, news, scandals, and recommendations. Ask if you can do a test project with the agency before committing to a full contract.

The Cost: Hybrid companies like this will cost a bit more than hiring a VA outright. That's because the agency does the work of vetting its assistants, training them, and handling administrative tasks like contracts and invoices. Usually, you can expect to pay between $5 and

$30 per hour more for a hybrid agency than for hiring an individual VA. As a business rule, agencies should be making a 50 percent profit margin on all clients so they can cover their expenses and grow. (That goes for you and your business, too!) That's the reason costs are higher. Also, hybrid agencies provide a layer of quality control and emergency support, so you're paying more for better, more reliable results.

Of course, cost always depends on whether the company has full-time employees or just contractors, whether they have any in-person physical offices to maintain, and whether there are any other overhead costs they need to account for like benefits. While I don't think you, as the client, need to understand how everyone creates their pricing structure, I do think it's helpful to understand why hybrid agencies are generally more expensive than standalone VAs.

For the remainder of this book, we are going to focus on the VA and the Hybrid model. You know, since that's my specialty and all. But I wanted to explain the different options here so you know about all the resources you have at your fingertips.

When it's time to let go and get your time back, there's no excuse for not hiring help. I promise you that when done right, the investment will pay off tenfold.

chapter eight

MEET YOUR VA SOULMATE

Finding your perfect virtual assistant is like finding your soulmate. We know it's possible because we have seen it happen, but we don't necessarily know how to get there. In my experience, finding your VA soulmate takes equal parts work and time. It also takes some soul-searching, which is why we started with the life audit. You can't find a good match if you can't be a good match. It takes two to tango, after all.

The obvious way to start narrowing down your options is to make sure that the people you're interviewing have the experience and skills that you've determined you need. In most cases, you don't want to have to train a person on how to do your assistant-worthy tasks, however I want to encourage you NOT to throw away a candidate if they don't have ALL the skills you need. You may do an interview with them and feel a kinship that you didn't feel with anyone else, which is often more important than the actual skills.

Why?

Because skills can be taught and learned, while personalities and attitudes cannot.

Make sure you're considering the entire package when you're looking at candidates:

- Past experience
- Skill set
- Vibes (Honestly, I know this sounds dumb, but your gut is a goddess and it's important to take her into account.)

Core Values All Great VAs Possess

Here's the reality: The hard skills it takes to be a great VA are always changing. (Or at least they are if you're a good VA who wants to keep up with the times!)

Podcasting becomes a thing, VAs learn how to produce podcasts. Content marketing explodes and VAs learn how to manage and edit blogs in WordPress.

These are two skills that I had to learn on the fly when my client said, "Hey Jess, I want to launch a podcast. Can you help me with that? Oh, and can you start managing the guest blog posts that are coming into my inbox every day?"

Perhaps foolishly, I said, "Sure!" and proceeded to spend an entire day Googling all the things about setting up, recording, producing, and publishing a new podcast as well as loading, editing, and scheduling blog posts in WordPress. At the time, there weren't courses or tutorials on any of this. I had to cobble together a bunch of articles from kind podcasting veterans.

Now, lucky for us, there are courses on everything you can imagine. There are even courses on how to make courses. Learning is easier than ever and great VAs take advantage of the wonderful world of knowledge we live in. (Spoiler alert: Curiosity and a willingness to learn are two of our core values!)

As long as the economy and the internet evolves, the virtual skills needed to help businesses grow will evolve as well. But if there's one thing I've learned over the years of coaching clients and assistants to make the perfect match, it's that the soft skills, personality traits, and core values that make up an outstanding VA are consistent across disciplines because the way the role works is consistent.

The VA who books your flights and the VA who researches your white paper content both need to have a few similarities in their attitude and approach in order to be successful.

1. Good Virtual Assistants Serve Without Ego.

This is the number one trait in a virtual assistant because they're always going to be just that: an assistant.

Unfortunately, I've seen too many people who want the work-at-home-flexible-schedule life but who are not comfortable working behind the scenes. They want to be out front getting all the credit for their work and they don't like situations where it's any other way. This will not work. The client (in this case YOU) is the star.

Humility In Action

Building up your personal brand is just as fulfilling to these assistants as building up their own brands. They get joy in seeing a client's following grow, or ghostwriting a blog post that gets featured in Forbes, or successfully booking a speaking gig that takes you to Madrid where you'll extend your trip and meet up with your spouse.

This Madrid extension was an actual project for one of our clients, and, lucky for me, coincided with a trip I was taking to Madrid. I was able to meet up with the client and her husband for happy hour. They were traveling with their daughter and I was with my fiance, so it was a total family affair! A perfectly serendipitous evening spending real-life quality time getting to know each other better personally, which is one of the best ways to maintain a positive relationship professionally.

That particular trip had several moving pieces and parts, but great VAs are known for accepting anything that is thrown at them with open arms. No task too big or too small for a humble assistant. In fact, small, seemingly menial tasks can be fun for them. They love responding to customer services emails under a generic account, making lunch reservations, and checking off the boxes on a to-do list. The only thing they love more than getting things done is making you happy.

Sort of like a puppy, but in virtual assistant form.

2. Good Virtual Assistants Provide Help With an Open Heart.

As I mentioned before, finding and growing the perfect virtual assistant relationship is not unlike nurturing any good relationship, whether it be a spouse or a friend.

Therefore, a great assistant has to care. At least a little bit at first. And then they have to be open to caring more as they start to get to know you better, just like a friend would, but in a professional way.

Theoretically, your virtual assistant has chosen this path as their career, so even though they don't see you in the office every day, their concern for your well-being is similar to that of colleagues in a face-to-face environment. Except it's actually better than that because you got to pick each other, whereas in an office setting you don't always get to choose your coworkers. Pretty cool, right?

Serving with an open heart means going the extra mile. It means crossing off tasks with a smile, offering words of kindness in an email exchange, and signing off with, "Have an awesome weekend!" on a Friday afternoon.

Eventually, it means reading in between the lines of what you're saying and finding solutions to problems you didn't even know you had.

A Neighborly Attitude in Action

When I say "neighborly" I don't necessarily mean extroverted. A neighborly attitude can come in all shapes and sizes.

It may mean sending you flowers when a family member dies. Or perhaps it's noticing that you asked for a flight to Chicago, but not a hotel, and offering to find one for you. You may not need it, but your neighborly assistant is always thinking. Just in case.

Another benefit of having a neighborly assistant is that you start to get to know each other personally. And you know what knowing someone builds? Trust. And trust is the number one barrier I see with clients who aren't able to build a successful relationship.

3. Good Virtual Assistants Take Initiative.

My previous point of noticing a missing link—a lack of a hotel reservation in the Chicago itinerary—is a great example of the next core value: initiative. It's one thing to notice that something is wrong or missing, it's another to offer to fix or add something to make it right.

Great virtual assistants don't sit around and wait for you to assign things. Sometimes this means being a little bit of a nag and saying things like, "Hey, I noticed we still haven't booked your flight for next month's trip. Are you ready to book? Here are a few options based on dates I pulled out of your calendar, but let me know if you'd rather leave or return on another date."

I really hate inefficient emails. I'd hate to say, "Are you ready to book that flight?" And then have to wait for my client to say, "Yes," before finding some flight options.

That's the difference between being proactive rather than reactive about something that has to get done.

In the flight example, I know they may not be ready to book yet for whatever reason, but I also know they NEED to book before prices go up and I don't want to get in trouble for booking a really expensive flight. As a result, I'm going to take that next step and make it easier for them to make a decision right now, when I need it.

In some ways, taking initiative is a little bit selfish from the assistant's part, at least in my case. (Don't tell!) But it doesn't present that way because it's actually really helpful for the client. Imagine that?

Proactivity In Action

There are few things I hate more than getting an email from a client that says something like, "How's that project going?"

I hate feeling like I'm not on top of things because, to me, if I'm not ahead of the curve I'm behind it. And no one likes being stuck behind the curve. If I get an email asking how something is going, that tells me that the person asking feels anxious about whether or not that project is going to get done on time, which is not good. Ugh, I'm getting twitchy just thinking about it!

To avoid that awful scenario, I send consistent updates on projects before my clients have to ask for them. I set the expectation that each week, I am going to send a report. The report will say, "Here are all the things I got done this week and here's what needs to get done next week." I know they didn't ask for this recap but I'm sending it anyway so they never have to wonder where I'm at.

(Also, it feels soooooo awesome to list out everything that got done and be like BAM! It's Friday and I'm a badass! You should try it sometime.)

A good assistant feels a nagging need to be proactive about projects and tasks because they're obsessed with keeping you in the loop. They lie awake at night wondering what else they can do to support you. Okay, maybe not every night. But remember, you are providing them with money, work, and a sense of purpose.

They don't take that for granted.

A great virtual assistant never twiddles their thumbs because they're always asking, "How can I help?"

4. Good Virtual Assistants Follow Through and Always Deliver on Time.

I'm shocked by the amount of people who tell me they tried to work with a freelancer or VA and could never get completed assignments back when they asked for them.

This blows my mind. As a VA, you literally have one job: do your work and deliver it when the client asks.

Now, sometimes there are extenuating circumstances for why projects get delivered late.

> 1. The client or the assistant misjudged the scope of the project and it's taking longer than budgeted.
> 2. The client or the assistant is missing a piece of the puzzle from someone else that is preventing the project from being finished on time.
> 3. Someone got sick or died.

Those are really the only reasons I can think of for a task or assignment not getting done on time and regardless of the reason, a change in timeline shouldn't be a surprise. If the issue is on the assistant's end, they need to give you a heads up that they're missing something, that they are running out of time, or that a family emergency has come up.

If it's on you as the client, you need to take the onus and provide a later deadline for whomever you're working with.

Either way, it does happen from time to time, but it should never happen for any other reason aside from one that's extenuating (and your contracts should state that).

Reliability In Action

You may have noticed that this core value is sort of a combo pack of proactivity and communication. A good virtual assistant takes pride in getting things done on time. Or foregoing the latest Netflix binge-session of

Stranger Things in favor of completing a work project. The feeling the assistant gets from reliably and kindly delivering something when it's asked for (if not early!) usurps most other priorities in their lives.

Great assistants double check their deadlines and deliverables. They put each task on their calendar or into their project management tool to ensure nothing gets lost. These assistants don't need to be reminded when something is due. They self-edit their work and they manage their time wisely.

Most people like to think of themselves as reliable, but there's a difference between doing what you say you're going to do eventually and doing what you say you're going to do on time.

5. Good Virtual Assistants Share Openly and Honestly.

Part of growing a positive relationship with your assistant is feeling confident that they will tell you things. Whether it's the fact that the price of a hotel went up overnight or that they'll be working from a lake house with slower wifi speed, strong communication skills must be one of their proudest skills.

This doesn't necessarily mean they went to college for PR or took a public speaking class. There are tons of different ways of communicating information honestly, for example, working as a cashier at a grocery store, as a hostess at a restaurant, or in any other customer-facing service role. These types of jobs require positive interactions with people on a daily basis and can be applied to an online assistant career.

The most important thing about your particular VA is that they communicate with you the way you like to be communicated with and they're not afraid to share all the information that's relevant to the task at hand.

Strong Communication In Action

Consistent, accurate updates are just the tip of the iceberg. These should be a given in any assistant relationship.

Strong communication for virtual assistants takes the whole status update thing to another level. Not only are these assistants eloquent in their writing (perhaps they have some perfectionist, Type A tendencies), but they are also efficient. They understand that you're busy, so they provide information in a way that is easy for you to consume.

Bullet-pointed lists of accomplishments with additional details if you choose to read them. Thoughtful recommendations on where to stay based on the type of fine dining experience they know you like to have. Information presented in a way that you can clearly understand, especially if you're in a rush.

Plus, of course, you want someone who is going to be straightforward about any impediments in their work. I can't tell you how many people have told me their virtual assistant "ghosted" on them. Why does this happen? Why can't we just communicate what's going on? Maybe a child is at home sick. Maybe there's an internet outage. Maybe a family member needed some emergency support.

Shit happens. Seriously. I say this all the time. We're not talking about rocket science or brain surgery. (You probably don't want a virtual assistant to help you in those industries.) And that's okay. Great virtual assistants are not afraid to tell you how their day is going or when they need help from you to succeed.

Just be wary of anyone who takes polite conversation to another level. Idle chit-chat or gossip that takes away from hours that could be spent on important work is a red flag.

6. Good Virtual Assistants Seek Opportunities to Learn and Grow.

After certain skills and experiences, this is the top request I get from prospective clients.

"I want someone who is going to be able to figure things out on their own. I don't want to have to show them how to do something every time."

My dear colleague, Jenn Hines, likes to say that she is the Queen of Googling. And I've seen this firsthand since the day she started as my virtual assistant.

Anytime I'd say, "Hey, I don't have time to do X. Can you figure it out and get back to me?" Within hours or even minutes, she'd come back with not one, but at least two or three ways to get it done so I could weigh in on which approach I preferred. Over time, she began to learn and internalize my decision-making process so she could simply present one idea, the one she knew I'd like best, and move forward.

Jenn is great at this because she is a sponge for knowledge. She just wants to know things. She wants to figure out problems and make them work.

Your assistant doesn't necessarily need to proclaim herself as the Queen of Googling, but she does need to know how to figure something out (whether it's by asking a colleague, doing a Google search, or going to a library) and take pride in implementing the knowledge she has gained.

Curiosity In Action

Curious assistants are known for the size of their bookshelves and the number of browser tabs they keep open at any given time. Their podcast queues are topped up with episodes of *Stuff You Should Know* and they're always asking their friends on Facebook what documentary they should watch next.

They like to know how things work for the sake of their own intelligence, but perhaps more importantly in this situation, they like to understand all options so they can choose the best one for you. Efficiency. It's the name of the game.

I recently interviewed someone who told me she loved reading SEO blogs because optimizing blog posts was like a game to her. We weren't even hiring an SEO person, but this anecdote told me she is someone who likes to figure things out. And yes, she was a bit nerdy. Which is also great!

While these types of people are comfortable finding information on their own, they also want to make sure they're satisfying your expectations. As a result, they're likely to ask a lot of questions. Don't take this as an indication that they don't know anything (unless they're asking stupid questions; know what they say about stupid questions and stupid people?). Take it as a sign that they aim to please and that they want to learn from you.

In the next section, I'll share some questions to ask and some red flags to look out for during the interview process so that you can make sure you're finding someone who meets these qualifications.

chapter nine

FACT-CHECK YOUR GUT INSTINCTS

You may be wondering how to find one of these magical unicorn VAs who possess all the lovely qualities I just mentioned. It probably feels you're Jack in *The Nightmare Before Christmas* and you're trying desperately to find the Christmas spirit inside a gloomy land of goblins, witches, and ghosts.

Just like everything else in business, finding an epically kind, communicative, curious, reliable, proactive, humble VA takes work. I want to ease the burden for you by offering a checklist that you can follow to make sure you're doing everything in your power to get the right person for the job.

You see, I don't want you to get stuck in the trap that I did when I first started hiring folks in 2011. I had no idea what I was doing when it came to hiring, I just knew I needed help. So like most baby entrepreneurs, I Googled "top interview questions" and "what to ask during an interview." I cobbled together some standard "what are your strengths and weaknesses" questions but it was all pretty lame in retrospect. Those generic questions didn't help me find the right people. Unsurprisingly, at that point in my life, just three years out of college, I had sat in the interviewee chair far more frequently than the interviewer chair.

Instead of only listening to my candidates' answers, I found myself watching their body language, examining their speech patterns, and noticing how I felt around them. The feeling was palpable regardless of whether we were doing an in-person interview or a video conference call.

What ended up being the most valuable for me in these interviews, as it turned out, was my gut.

And that's all well and good. Sometimes you just have a feeling about someone, they're perfect for what you've been looking for, and you can tell that they're up for the job.

But . . . well . . . guts can be finicky. And that thing they say about going with your gut because your gut is always right? Not true.

The first full-time contractor I hired was a total bust. I had a great time meeting with her, talking to her about her experience, and learning about her passions. She was charismatic, had a lot of the kinds of experiences I was hiring for, and really seemed excited about the work.

I wanted to hire her on the spot, but I gave myself a night to sleep on it before extending the offer. I didn't check her references, I didn't ask for any kind of work examples outside of a normal cover letter and resume, and the relationship fell on its face in less than a year.

Letting her go was one of the worst things I've ever had to do in my business. I felt cheated. I felt duped. I felt like I had put my delicate trust in someone who just threw it in the garbage without so much as a backward glance.

When I reset the password to her email so I could go in and finish the projects she had barely started, the web of lies and lack of progress revealed themselves further and I began wallowing in a pit of despair.

It took quite a while for me to recover from that, and even now, I'm very slow to hire. I never want to find myself in that sad, sorry place where I felt betrayed by my team member and worse, by my own gut.

I vowed to create a more concrete process that wouldn't leave anything to chance. This process would validate or deny my gut feeling.

Step 1: Conduct The Interview

Most people, as it turns out, have never had to hire or fire anyone. They're not in that department.

If you're looking to hire some virtual support, you're now in the position of making a big important hiring decision. The best thing you can do is be prepared by arming yourself with the right questions and the right evaluation points to weed out anyone who isn't a fit.

You'll want to review the candidate's materials closely before you choose to take the next step and interview them, of course. The resume, cover letter, and any past testimonials should be able to tell you whether they have the skills to do what you need. The interview should be used to get a better sense of who the person is and whether you think they'll be a good match for you long-term. It's a bit of a personality test mixed with a communications gauge and, of course, a gathering of the vibes. I'm all about the good vibes!

When you schedule the interview, pay attention to how the candidate answers your questions and how long it takes them to respond. I believe the interview starts the second they fill out your application and all of the communication from that point on is part of your evaluation process.

Try to conduct the interview using a video conferencing service like Zoom, Google Hangouts, or Skype. Notice if there is any push back to this, whether it's related to an unwillingness to try video or to a technological issue. Also, try to arrive to the interview right on time and see if the candidate is already there waiting for you.

Punctuality is paramount.

Once you get settled in with your notebook and pen (or Google Doc/Evernote notebook/Word doc), you can ease into the interview with some niceties, an explanation of whatever's behind you, or a close-up of your hamster.

You set the tone of the interview and you have the opportunity to give your candidate a real first impression of who you are. Make sure it's a positive one. They get to choose you just as much as you get to choose them.

Common interview questions include:

- What do you see as your biggest strength?
- What is something you're working on? (A ploy to figure out someone's "weaknesses" without saying it.)
- Where do you see yourself in five years?
- Why do you want this job?
- What is your biggest professional achievement?

And so on.

There are also some questions that work specifically for virtual support and for finding candidates that have those six core values that we talked about earlier. In addition to sharing the questions and why they're important, I'll also share some positive qualities to pay attention to as well as some red flags.

Remember that none of these questions are make-or-breaks on their own. A candidate might show some signs of the red flags but still be a great fit. Instead, the answers to these questions are meant to provide some food for thought as you're making your decision.

1. What's your story?

I love starting any interview with an open-ended question, particularly this one. I'll usually preface it by letting the candidate know I did in fact read their resume and cover letter, I'm not being a lazy jerk, but I love to hear about what they're doing in their own words.

These kinds of questions allow your candidate to ease into the interview (after all, what they've been doing with their life thus far shouldn't be a hard question to answer) and it gives you a peek into the way they speak and articulate themselves.

This question is actually SO open-ended that they can take it in a variety of different ways. Take note of which direction they choose to go. Do they tell you about the day they were born? What their family and growing up was like? Do they stick to the last few years of their professional life? Do they get choked up and confused?

Since strong communication skills are so important, and should be evaluated throughout the entire interview, starting out with a longer, explanatory answer is useful. Plus, open-ended questions require a certain level of creativity and confidence.

It's a simple question, but can reveal a complicated set of traits and values about a potential hire.

Follow-Up Questions:

- **What was that like?** I have interviewed some extremely interesting people with insane former job titles and experiences. It's great to expand on certain areas of past experiences if you're interested, whether it applies to the position or not. It's another way to get the candidate to feel comfortable and engaged in the interview.

- **How did you find me?** Sometimes people put a referral source on their application or cover letter and sometimes they don't. It's great to hear where someone came from so you can thank the connection or find out more.
- **What made you decide to apply for this position?** Sometimes it will be obvious from the answer to the previous question, but if it's not, this is a good thing to know.

Things to Pay Attention To:

- Any mention of skills or experiences that directly relate to the job you're hiring.
- A conscious effort to tie in how they found you or what brought them to this point in their career.
- Keeping it positive, even if they hated their last position. You don't want someone who is a gossip or who goes around bad-mouthing employers. That could be you one day!

Red Flags:

- Little or no experience working in an assistant capacity. Sometimes I get candidates who are overqualified for the position. They've had a ton of experience, but have been in more of a managerial level. Now, they might be starting a family or wanting a career change. But it's a red flag because they may be too used to the power that comes with being the manager as opposed to the different power dynamic of being an assistant. Of course, this isn't always the case. I have a great VA on my team who had been working on her own strategy business for years before she found Don't Panic Management. She had done all of the implementation work before in other roles, decided to focus on the strategic side when she launched her company, but realized she preferred being in the weeds, doing the work. Her priorities had shifted, she was able to explain what she wanted at that point, so in this particular situation her experience was not a red flag at all.

- Short, vague answers that don't reveal anything particularly useful about the candidate's experiences or their personality. This tells me that their communication skills may not be very strong or that they weren't prepared for the interview. Look, everyone knows that when you're an interview candidate you're going to be put on the spot and it's your time to shine in the spotlight. If you don't have anything to say about yourself, well . . . I call bullshit! There are ways for candidates to figure out what they're best at, what colleagues have said about their experiences of working with them in the past, and what makes them light up at the end of a hard day. There's no excuse for not having prepared something interesting to talk about during an interview. While it's not necessary for them to be great storytellers, being able to speak about themselves and their experiences is particularly important if you're interviewing for a marketing-related position. Many marketing tasks require a level of creativity and storytelling, so it's vital to look for this in the interview.

- Of course, if the candidate doesn't have the experience in the type of work you're looking for, you should see that on their resume. Don't schedule an interview with someone who has never done the type of work you need unless they've been specifically referred to you as someone who's a fast learner!

2. Have you ever worked remotely before?

This question is so obvious I almost didn't even write it down. But you'd be surprised by how many folks think they can work from the comfort of their own home and are quickly awakened by the rude and difficult truth that it's not so easy.

If you've never worked remotely, you don't realize how much discipline it takes. No one is watching over your shoulder making sure you're getting your tasks done and no one is keeping you from turning on the TV or cleaning the dishes.

No one is making you stick to a certain schedule or take a lunch break.

Oftentimes, unless you work in a shared co-working space or coffee shop, no one is there for you to talk to.

The lack of structure is a huge barrier for many people to overcome and they soon find that they're not actually disciplined enough to make it work. They need the office environment with its accountability to be productive.

I've heard too many stories of work-at-home depression that comes from not recognizing how isolating it is before taking the plunge.

Follow-Up Questions:

- **What does a typical schedule or routine look like for you during your work day?** You don't want to make people feel defensive here or like one way is better than the other, so it's a good idea to keep this question as open-ended as possible. Remember, unless you are hiring for an employee relationship, you can't require your virtual support to work certain hours. Labor laws make clear distinctions between and employees and contractors. This question is meant to gauge their work style and give you a sense of whether or not it works with yours. For example, you might be an early riser who loves to watch three episodes of *Gilmore Girls* before you start your workday in New York. Someone in California who binge-watches *Scandal* in the afternoon and tends to work nights might be a great fit for you because they'd have their work completed and in your inbox at the end of their night on the west coast by the time you're up and working on the east coast.

- **What kinds of technology do you use to communicate remotely?** Ideally, you're already on a video call with your candidate, but it's important for you to know if they've had experience with other virtual communication tools such as Slack, Skype, Zoom, Sococo, and Google Chats.

- **If they have worked remotely before: What are your biggest challenges working remotely?** This can be hilarious. I've heard crazy stories about dogs, babies, and significant others, as well as yard work and demolition projects next door. But what you're looking for here is a window into the personality of your candidate. Is it hard for them to get out of bed? To remember to eat? (I have both of these problems.) Or perhaps they're challenged by separating work life from home life and they tend to work 12-hour days because the computer is right there. (I have this problem, too.) Digging deeper here gives you a sense of their vulnerabilities so you can be sensitive to them if and when you decide to work together. It also shows you how open and honest they're willing to be in an initial conversation. You want to hear a tactful response, not an embarrassing one.

- **If they haven't worked remotely before: What challenges do you foresee when it comes to working remotely?** And they better have an answer here. If they're like, "Weeeee I get to go to Starbucks four times a day and eat all the cheetos on my couch!" Then you know you've got a slacker on your hands. If they recognize, for example, that they're an extrovert and will need to find some sort of co-working situation to make them successful, that shows you that they are self-aware and understanding that remote work can be tough depending on what kind of person you are.

Things to Pay Attention To:

- Having remote experience is definitely a big plus, but it's not necessary. You'll have to decide how important this is to you, but keep in mind that you may want to provide some supporting resources for them if they have not worked in a virtual environment before.
- Honesty about any challenges or potential setbacks.
- Experience using technology to communicate virtually.

Red Flag:

- No prior remote work experience is a red flag, but it's not necessarily a deal-breaker. It's more about the personality of the assistant and whether you're willing to work with them on making sure they have the resources they need to be successful in a virtual environment.

3. Tell me about a time when you crushed it so hard at work that you wanted to go screaming from the rooftops about how much you rock.

People experience a sense of accomplishment in different ways. For some, it could mean simply finishing a project on time and getting a thumbs up from a boss. For others, it could be helping to solve a conflict between coworkers. Still others might like to see their name emblazoned on a trophy for getting the most steps on their FitBit that month.

My absolute favorite answer ever to this question was one that my Chief People Officer, Becca, received from a potential assistant last year. It cracked us up then and continues to make us giggle every time we think about it. Becca was conducting the first-round interview when she asked this question and the answer went something like this:

It was this particular assistant's first job out of college and she had been hired for a pretty standard assistant-type role. On one of her first days, the team asked her to make some coffee for a big staff meeting. Shockingly, she had never done this before and was panicked about what she would do.

Hiding in the break room, she frantically called her mom and asked her to walk her through the steps of making a pot of coffee. (Oh, if I had a dime for all the times I've called my mom to ask her how to do some adult-worthy task, we'd all be rich!)

She made the coffee and brought it into the meeting. She felt pretty good about her big accomplishment. But she noticed that while the team had all poured themselves a cup, no one touched their mugs after the first sip. And as she was cleaning up after the meeting, she found herself throwing away mug after mug full of coffee left by the team.

It was nice that they didn't throw her shade for making a truly terrible pot of coffee.

That night, she went home, mortified, and made about a dozen pots of coffee, forcing a taste of each one to her roommate who gave her notes about what was wrong and what was right. She continued this process until she successfully made a normal-ass pot of coffee that she'd be able to recreate on the job the next meeting.

I love this story for a few reasons. One, it's hilarious. I can just imagine her excitement when she gets the coffee going followed by her sad, sad disappointment when no one can stomach it. Two, it shows an eagerness to work hard to do a good job, no matter what the task is. And three, it shows resilience. Was she dissuaded by her poor coffee-making skills? Did she go cry in a corner, cursing her entire college education for not teaching her how to make one delicious godforsaken pot of coffee? No! She went home, turned on a coffee maker, and practiced until she got it right.

Hearing and understanding what makes an assistant proud can help inform how you reward them for a job well done. People need to feel appreciated in order to have job satisfaction, and as the manager, that part is on you.

On the other hand, if all they care about is public recognition and vacation time, you'll know that you may not have the most humble assistant on your hand and they may not be the best fit.

Follow-Up Question:

- **What's your favorite part of your (current or former) job?** If you can get a straight answer here you'll start to get to the core of what your candidate is all about. You'll also be able to start to envision how they'll be able to work for you. Do they love compiling spreadsheets? Awesome. Do they love color-coding the meeting schedule? Super awesome. Do they love picking out where they're going to eat lunch each day? Maybe not as awesome, although finding and booking restaurants could be part of the job!

Red Flag:

- If your candidate shares a time when they were awarded publicly for something they did and that's the part that made them feel the most satisfied, you may be dealing with someone who is too praise-focused for a behind-the-scenes role. The reality of the virtual assistant experience is that it's pretty un-glamorous. The type of people who thrive are the ones who don't need a whole lot of direction or a whole lot of praise for their work. They are satisfied by simply delivering a good product on time, not being coddled with "this is awesome and here's a prize"-type feedback. Now, this doesn't mean you should stop giving just as much positive feedback, if not more, than negative, but you shouldn't work with someone who can only feel good about their work when someone else recognizes it.

4. Tell me about a time when you made a mistake. What happened and how did you handle it?

I love this question because it's another one that can go in a number of ways. First, see how long it takes them to come up with an example. In my experience, the ones who are quick to pull something out of a hat are the ones who possess more attention to detail and are more eager to please. They internalize even the simplest of mistakes and work to remedy them as soon as possible.

Regardless of how long it takes for them to find an example, listen to the part about how they handled the mistake very closely. More often than not, especially in virtual assistant land, the mistake is not a big deal. It's about how they handled it. Because let's be honest: they ARE going to make mistakes. Everyone does. But you'll need to figure out how they'll make it right, especially if you're not there to notice or reprimand them (because you're so busy and all).

In the best scenarios, an assistant will not only tell you about the mistake, but they will have already fixed it and come up with a solution to make sure it doesn't happen again.

In the worst scenarios, an assistant either doesn't recognize the mistake or worse, hides the mistake, letting you find out about it later from a colleague, fan, or follower.

Ugh, I shudder to think about that, especially as someone who has experienced it firsthand.

This question helps you gauge whether you're dealing with someone who could put you or your business in a compromising situation.

Follow-Up Question:

- **What did you learn from this experience?** You want to get to the heart of whether this person is proactive about finding solutions even in the face of disaster. Can they keep calm, cool, and collected when something goes wrong? Do they do a healthy amount of reflection if and when something does go wrong (because it will) and then determine a system to make sure it doesn't happen again?

Red Flag:

- A lack of acknowledgement of the mistake. This really aggravates me and ties into the entitlement issue that a need for praise often indicates. The best virtual assistants take ownership for a mistake even if they know it's not their fault. That's because it's their job to keep projects moving forward and make things right for their client, no matter what. If you don't get the sense that this candidate would be willing to fall on their sword for you, you may not be working with someone who will be a good long-term fit. (But, for the record, just because they *will* fall on their sword doesn't mean you should ever let them. Everyone needs to own up to a mistake when they make one— even you!)

5. Let's say we started working together today. One year from now, what do you think I'd have to say in a testimonial about you?

This question tests your candidate's appetite for forward-thinking reflection. It also sets the expectation that you do intend to measure the success of the relationship over time and that it's something they'll need to work on with you.

You want to see the wheels turning here. Taking a pause to think about this one is totally fine. This is the question that reveals what they really think about themselves and their work.

Follow-Up Questions:

- What have other people said is their favorite part about working with you?

- **Are there things that you've done to make sure you're performing well at your job?** This follow-up is more relevant for people who have worked as a virtual assistant before. Since virtual assistants are responsible for growing and maintaining their own client base, it's important for them to be checking in and making sure their clients are happy. You'll want to be giving feedback and having review meetings as the manager, of course, but it's great when you can see an assistant taking the initiative to ensure that they are providing a great service.

Red Flags:

- If they give vague and vapid answers like, "I'm really nice," or they can't be specific about the kinds of things that you'll love about working with them, they may not be confident in their abilities, they may not be a very good communicator, or it might be a combination of the both.
- On the contrary, if they're saying things like, "I'M GONNA CHANGE YOUR LIFE, YO!" then they may be overly confident and you really don't want that either. The balance is in the humility. Confidence without cockiness. It's a delicate line to walk, but you'll be able to see the signs throughout the interview and decide accordingly.

6. What do you do to keep learning?

Perhaps my favorite question of all time, this one teaches you about whether or not your candidate is that master of curiosity. That Google-queen who we all covet.

Most commonly, I'll get answers like, "I read a lot," or, "I listen to a lot of podcasts." This is great if you can dig deeper into what types of content they consume. Romance novels and the *Welcome to Night Vale* podcast are all well and good for their entertainment value, but a perfect answer involves something about seeking answers and gaining knowledge simply for the sake of it. It shows you they have an active mind and that personal growth is important to them.

Follow-Up Question:

- **What are your favorite TV shows/movies/ books/podcasts?** If you have time, seeing if you have any common ground in the types of media you like to consume can be a great way to build rapport with your candidate. Ultimately, commonalities can also help us trust each other, kickstarting that deeper connection which leads to a long-lasting relationship.

Red Flag:

- If the person you're interviewing doesn't have any hobbies or doesn't seem excited to talk to you about their interests and knowledge, they may be fine to do menial and very objective tasks, but they may not be what you need to help you grow your business. That is completely up to you. The type of work you need done COULD indeed be perfect for a simple, quiet person. But in my experience, you want someone with life in their eyes, someone who craves knowledge, who loves solving problems, and desires growth.

No one question should be the crown jewel of your interview. Make sure you take notes throughout your interview, record it if you can, and take a holistic look at your candidates' answers before you make a decision.

Remember, you don't have to choose just one candidate at this point. If possible, depending on your timeline, you'll be able to pick your top two or three candidates and have them do a test project for you. Then you'll be able to make an educated choice about which one is best for you.

In the next section, we'll discuss some strategies for assigning and evaluating test projects, followed by a training procedure that doesn't make you want to bury your face in the sand like a sad, sad ostrich.

Step 2: Administer The Test

I believe that all great working relationships start with a test. Maybe even all great relationships period. I remember lots of times when I put my poor boyfriend through all kinds of tests. Like when I would ask him if he wanted to go meet my college friends at a club (he hates big crowds and loud music) or when I hinted at a new hiking spot we should check out (he hates walking around outside for no reason) or when I made shrimp for dinner and said, "Is it goooooood?" (he hates shellfish). He needed to prove that he loved me and trusted me and cared about the things I cared about (or at least pretended to) so that we could continue to trust each other over time. (Spoiler alert: He passed. And is now my fiancé.)

Think of the virtual assistant test like a supplement to your application process. Or part two of your interview process. If you're going to go out on a limb with someone, they need to show you what they're made of.

Your VA is not exactly your spouse, of course, but you'll be relying on them day in and day out, trusting them with your precious details, and sharing your deepest preferences with them. It is, or should be, one of your most coveted relationships.

Now, the type of test project you choose to create should depend on the type of assistant you're looking for. Need a copywriter? Create a blog writing assignment. Need a more generalized admin? Create a fake (or heck, even a real) trip that you need lots of planes, trains, and automobiles booked for.

Regardless of what the actual test project is, make sure it meets the following requirements:

- Comes with specific outcomes
- Has a clear deadline
- Is able to be evaluated/measured

You'll also need to decide if you want to pay for test projects or not. I've heard an argument for both sides:

1. Jess, you just said this is part of the application/interview process and I don't pay people to go through that.
2. Work is work, whether it's being used as a test or in an actual situation, and people deserve to get paid for their work.

I see both points of view here, but in my opinion, even if you only have a small amount of money to throw at two or three test projects, you're better off. You'll show good faith to your candidates, and, if you use a test project that's a real assignment, you'll get some quality work out of it.

A per-assignment payment of $25 or $50 could do the trick. So even if you have three candidates and you pay them $50 each, you're out $150, but you've found your perfect match. I only wish choosing your soulmate from a dating pool were this easy!

Let's take the example of someone applying to be an administrative VA. I wanted to share an actual project brief of what a test project might look like so you can get a sense of what you might want yours to look like. I've included full details, email templates, and rubrics in the appendix that you can steal as well.

Project Type: Executive Assistance
Fee: $75
Approximate time: 3 hours
Project Description: Research 5 potential speaking

gigs and 10 potential podcast gigs for Jess. Compile your research in a Google sheet with all important data (contact info, application deadlines, etc). Then, create Asana tasks and calendar appointments to remind her about any submission deadlines.

Measurement: Compare against one month of our internal assistant's work (who does this on a regular basis).

Skills Tested: Calendar management, research, project management

You'll notice that this particular project is actually useful to me, though again, it could be a totally fake or arbitrary assignment. It's easiest to create one test project per type of work so you don't have to reinvent the wheel every time you want to hire someone new. Whether that be a back-burner ongoing project or a project that you need done periodically, try to make your life easier by only creating these projects once!

When you send an email asking your candidate to perform this test, make sure the email is specific and clear. You want to test this new assistant's ability to follow directions and complete a project on time. You do not want to test their mind-reading skills. Eventually, it's every assistant's goal to be able to read your mind and tell the future. But not today, pal, not today.

Don't leave anything open for interpretation or chance. Do be available for clarifying questions from your candidate. When I see someone who responds in a timely manner with something like, "Thanks so much for this! I believe I have everything I need to get this done and you'll have it in your inbox by [DATE]," I'm stoked.

Alternatively, if I get something like, "Hey there! I had a few questions about this." I'm also stoked. I'd rather get the questions up front. It shows me that they've read the assignment thoroughly (most of the time, unless their questions are literally answered in the assignment; that's a fail) and that they are not waiting until the last minute to review.

There's something about setting expectations and keeping everyone on the same page that does wonders for future outcomes. Remember when I forced my quiet, jazz-loving fiancé into a club full of tequila shots and booty-shaking beats? I promised him he only had to stay for an hour and he agreed that if I wasn't ready to leave by the time he was, we'd meet at home.

I got what I wanted—time for him to meet my friends and experience a taste of my college life. He got what he wanted—a happy fiancée and an early bedtime. So even though we both didn't want the same things that night, our clear expectations allowed us to compromise and remain satisfied with the outcome of the night.

So, again, not *exactly* the same as testing your VA, but not so far off if you look at it from a high level.

Once you've received your test projects, you need a rubric or system to evaluate their work. You can always just pick whichever one had the best hairstyle on the interview call, but that's not so fair (and is also probably an HR violation for everyone except someone who runs a hair salon).

If you're anything like me, you like to give people the benefit of the doubt in the beginning. Aw, she didn't realize I meant Google Docs, not Word. Aw, he didn't see that little typo right there. It's fine. They'll get better.

No! There are a billion fish in the sea (very scientific, I know) and if someone can't follow your very specific directions, you need to find someone who can.

At Don't Panic Management, we use a rubric to evaluate test projets. The rubric utilizes a red, yellow, green system for much of what we do and it really helps us attach an objective value to an otherwise subjective process.

Each color is associated with a number (red = 1, yellow = 2, green = 3), and so we are able to add up those numbers and give the person a score by the end of the process. Check out the full rubric in the appendix and feel free to adapt it for your own projects!

No matter how you evaluate projects, make sure you actually do evaluate them with some sort of system. You don't want to hire someone on a hunch and a referral and call it a day. You want to make sure that if nothing else, they can follow directions and deliver work on time. Skills can easily be trained. Punctuality and strong communication skills are much harder.

Step 3: Negotiate Retainers & Rates

There are a lot of discussions around the topic of payment for VA relationships.

A lot of people like to pay by the hour. You turn in a timesheet at the end of the week and that's the tally of your progress. You work an hour, you get paid for an hour.

Personally, I don't find this approach to be very useful. It focuses more on the process than the product. Plus, it's a lot of administrative time to track and review a timesheet each week.

I would much prefer to see results!

Sure, someone could be sitting at their computer working on thinking about working on a project and then charge me for that. Alternatively, we could agree on a guideline of hours for each project, a set of deliverable expectations, and call it day. In this way, the assistant may use up all the hours perfectly as expected or not. But you're protected from having them bill you for way more hours than anticipated and they're protected from making less money because they can deliver a quality product in less time than expected.

I always recommend tracking hours even if you're not paying by the hour so that you can see if your estimates are on or off the mark. An assistant isn't going to want to continue working with you if they're consistently spending 20 hours on a project that should take ten. Likewise, if they're grossly underutilizing the hours allocated to a project, you could be wasting your money. You never want to waste money that you could be using to invest in other parts of your business. Or, you know, money you could be using to buy cheese.

Ongoing evaluation of how long assignments take and whether your VA is meeting your expectations is just plain smart. I suggest scheduling a weekly or monthly retainer and deliverables review so you can see how it's going.

The retainer you set up with your VA could look something like this:

Work Type	Retainer	Monthly Rate	Hourly Rate
Virtual Assistance	5 hours/week	$860 / month	$40
Podcast Production	4 episodes/month	$1,290 /month	$60
TOTALS	5 Hours/Week + 4 Episodes/Month	$2,150	

Or like this:

Work Type (Beginning Dec 1, 2017)	Retainer	Monthly Rate	Hourly Rate
Community Management	12 Hours/Week	$2,838	$55
Content Management	15 Hours/Week	$3,870	$60
Virtual Assistance	5 Hours/Week	$860	$40
TOTAL	32 Hours/Week	$7,568	

If you don't have consistent work like this, most people will pay a flat project rate. They'll send 50 percent of the payment up front and 50 percent upon completion. As always, you'll need to negotiate this with your assistant and remember that they are the boss of their own operation, so they may have their own payment terms that you'll need to consider.

Now, let's talk about costs.

chapter ten

IT'S NOT ALL ABOUT THE BENJAMINS

Virtual assistants can cost anywhere from $3 per hour to $300 per hour. I'm serious. It all depends on their experience, where they live, and what their skills are.

When I started working as Jay's VA back in 2010, he sent me an email to ask me what my rates were. As you should when you're hiring someone. I laughed out loud when I received that email. Ha! I had no idea what a virtual assistant was before I saw his tweet, let alone what to charge. I searched executive assistant salaries, cost of living in LA, and found a calculator tool for determining a reasonable hourly rate. I'm pretty sure it was $10 per hour.

That was a good start. But, of course, I had never been a contractor before. I didn't know that I had to pay for my own equipment, my own technology, and oh yeah, my own health insurance and a 401k.

I had massively undervalued myself and my needs at the time, but the truth was I didn't need much. I was still under my mom's insurance until I was 26 (thanks, Obama!) and was still shopping at Trader Joe's (although I didn't qualify for food stamps anymore, yayyyyy!). I lived in a four-bedroom apartment with three roommates, so my rent and expenses were low.

As far as a good time for getting my feet wet in a new industry goes, this was pretty perfect. I didn't have any significant others or dependents to worry about. I didn't have any pets. I had a roof over my head, food on the table, insurance in case I got sick, and lots of family and friends to take care of me if something went wrong. Going to Venice Beach to lay by the waves and listen to the street musicians was free. A couple bucks to tip the performers and buy a new pair of sunglasses was all I needed.

Ahh, those were the good old days.

Over time, I was able to, you know, begin to become an adult. The more skills I acquired, the more I was able to charge. Over time, I could present higher rates to new clients and raise my rates with current clients, but I had to start somewhere. As do you!

The best way to determine what you should pay for a virtual assistant (and what you can afford) is to ask yourself a few questions:

1. How Much Can I Comfortably Invest Each Month?

I had to put "invest" in this question because yes, hiring a virtual assistant is an investment. It's an investment in your business, but perhaps more importantly, it's an investment in yourself. You are spending money to give yourself some freedom. The freedom to do the things you love and the freedom to grow. If you can wrap your head around the concept, you'll value your virtual assistant, and when they feel valued, they perform better for you. Imagine that!

Start by looking at your budget.

If you're an intrapreneur (and you totally are if you're working for a company but looking toward innovative ways of getting work done, you smarty pants, you), then you may have a set budget that's been allocated by your boss or department head for hiring external vendors. This situation actually makes things easier in some ways because you know exactly what you can spend and what your parameters are regardless of whether you like it or not.

(Hopefully, in the future, you can lobby for more money because your new VA proves to be so helpful.)

On the entrepreneur side of the equation, there are more factors to consider.

If you're an entrepreneur, you'll want to look at all of your income and expenses, plus any money you're setting aside for things like retirement, savings, college funds, custom sneakers, cheese, whatever. You'll also want to look at your cash reserve and growth goals. Sometimes you have to spend money to make money, but you want to be a little more conservative at first so you don't drain your business of all its operating budget.

I recommend consulting with a CPA and/or hiring a CFO to help you make financial decisions, especially if you don't feel particularly comfortable knowing what's smart (i.e., you are like most people and don't have a finance degree or you haven't managed businesses in the past).

When it was just me and my LLC, I could easily see the month's expenses and income because there were only a few streams going in and out of the bank account. Now, I work with a company called Summit CPA (http://summitcpa.net). They've been instrumental in helping me make sure I'm set up as the right entity, organizing my books at a new level, and generally making me understand my finances so I can make sound decisions.

These days, payroll, taxes, technology costs, retainers, travel, meals, and everything in between no longer keep me awake at night. I have someone watching the accounts all the time and providing accountability on growth goals, cash reserve goals, and profit margin goals.

As with hiring a VA, hiring a CPA or CFO doesn't have to be a big investment. You can use virtual help here, too. (Summit's entire team is virtual, for example, and I'd be happy to make an intro to them!)

Once you've determined what your budget looks like, figure out a monthly fee that you can comfortably set aside for a virtual assistant.

2. Does This Rate Seem Reasonable?

Once you have your monthly budget set out, compare it against your list of all the things you want to delegate.

If you have $1,000 per month to spend on an assistant and you have ten hours per week of work that you need to delegate, that means $250 per week / ten hours per week = $25 per hour.

Is $25 per hour reasonable? Yes. You will be able to get a very good virtual assistant for this rate.

Let's say you have $2,000 per month to spend on an assistant and you've got ten hours per week of work that you need to delegate. Even better. You can either get a better quality assistant at a higher rate to do more deep, important work for you, or you can double the amount of hours you want to delegate. Or, and this is what I would do, spend half of it now on your ten-hours-per-week assistant, see how it goes, and then you've got room to grow if you're finding success in the relationship.

On the other hand, if you only have $300 per month to invest but you need ten hours per week of support, you'll end up with an assistant that's charging around $7.50 per hour. Now, that might seem sufficient to you if you've got some very basic, foolproof data entry or the like. But you most likely will not be able to find someone in the states or Europe for that rate. If that's not important to you, great! This is still a reasonable figure for you.

It's all about your priorities and values. There's no correct answer here. It's whatever feels most reasonable to you.

3. How Much Time Am I Willing to Spend?

Investing in virtual support is not only a monetary commitment. It's also an investment in your time and energy, which, just like money, is finite (for most of us, at least).

Finding a great assistant who actually wants to work for you is half of the battle for achieving that coveted state of calm. The other half is on you. The amount of time you put into training, nurturing, and providing feedback for your assistant will directly translate into how successful you are at working together.

Great assistants thrive on doing good work and making you happy. You will, eventually, thrive on having someone on your side that you trust to do your assignments thoroughly and on time. Fortunately or unfortunately, getting to that point requires time and effort on your part.

If you're so bogged down that you know you can't spend a few hours each week talking to your assistant, walking them through projects and expectations, reviewing their work, and thinking up new assignments for next week, you may not be ready for a VA. And that's okay! You'll be better off waiting until you've cleared a few things off your plate or performed some magic to create more hours in the day.

At the same time, it's possible that if you delegate a few big assignments that you've been spending a lot of your time on, you can ease into the relationship by getting those big projects off your plate pretty much immediately. This way, you can have the time back in your day to work with your assistant on more ongoing projects.

I know, you're probably thinking, "this sounds hard." Well, yeah! It *is* hard. If it were easy, everyone would be doing it. And everyone would have a success story to report. But that's not the case. When we forget that our assistants need us just as much as we need them, we neglect our own future and we set ourselves up for failure.

Don't overlook the monetary *and* time investments required to make this work.

Step 4: Create a Contract

You have your candidate lined up and ready to go. Their test project was stellar. You're feelin' funky fresh and ready to rock!

Handshake agreements are great, but written and signed contracts are better. If you've worked with contractor-type relationships before, you may already have an agreement in place. If not, read on for some specifics about what to include in a virtual assistant agreement.

Not only will this help keep you from getting burned, but like a prenup, this will make you feel more comfortable and safe within the relationship.

Important note: It's no secret that I'm not a lawyer. Fun fact: I did do my work study program at the NYU School of Law but that doesn't count for anything in this case. The ideas below include important contract elements, as recommended by my lawyer. Always make sure you pass any legal documents by your own lawyer before putting them out into the world.

Description of Services

No agreement is complete without an outline of what is being agreed upon.

Make sure you list out all the tasks or categories of tasks that you expect your assistant to complete. Leave room for a statement like "and other administrative duties as needed" so that you have some room to expand if it fits within the scope of hours you've hired for.

Also consider what the terms of changing the description of services might be. For Don't Panic, we have an agreement with our clients that they must provide 30-day written notice if they want to change their services. Of course, if it's something basic within the scope of what we are already doing and doesn't add or remove any hours, it's no big deal. But the reason we have those terms in our client contracts is because we have a similar term agreement with our assistants. For them, it's a 14-day written notice.

Having a buffer between the 30 days from the client and the 14 days for the assistant is really important for us to be able to deliver what's needed while still being decent people. I know this isn't a requirement, but I would never want to kick an assistant to the curb without notice just because a client's scope of work changed or they got sick or was dealing with any other unforeseen circumstance.

Make sure you protect yourself and your work by including scope of work change terms here.

Payment Terms and Compensation

How much will you pay your assistant and when will you pay them?

This is the stuff that contracts are made for, right? Cue Tom Cruise yelling, "Show me the moneyyyyy!!!"

When you're dealing with contractors or freelancers, you may need to negotiate this because they sometimes have (and are entitled to) their own terms of payment. For example, if your arrangement has the assistant sending an invoice when work has been complete and the invoice payment is due within 30 days according to the assistant (who is the service provider here) then those are your payment terms.

If you're not comfortable with that arrangement, it's worth a conversation with the assistant to see if you can find a mutually agreeable situation that fits within your own expected payment terms.

Don't Panic invoices on the first of the month and payment is due by the end of that month for work performed during the month. This is a standard agency procedure and we decided that it was the best model for us.

Now, I've gotten push back on this in the past. For example, I've had clients ask if they can pay weekly instead. My answer was no, I'm not going to send you an invoice every week. But! You can make partial payments against the monthly invoice I send so that it's like you're paying a new invoice every week. That's your prerogative.

What do I care as long as the invoice is fully paid by the end of the month?

You will need to decide how important payment terms are to you and whether or not you're willing to budge on them. If you know you're pretty strict about how you want to pay people, it's worth discussing during the interview process, especially if you're chatting with someone you really like. You don't want to get into a situation where you're going to start working with someone whose payment structure doesn't work for you.

Don't Panic also has a rule about checks. We don't accept paper checks because we are fully distributed (which means that our entire team works virtually) and don't have a reliable way to receive and cash them. I refuse to give my home address out to clients (unless I've known them for a while and they are sending me wine). This is a problem for some people. They can't understand why we don't do business this way.

I get it. I really do. But, and this is a bigger point that we'll dive into more later, we had to streamline our invoicing and payment system as we grew because we couldn't sustain having a different process for each client.

Efficiency. It's all about efficiency in everything we do. We need to be efficient in our systems and processes, otherwise we can't scale.

In addition to deciding how much and when you'll pay your assistant, you will also need to be explicit about any situations in which you will *not* pay, such as not performing the services to completion or not performing them to your level of satisfaction.

Other things you may want to include here:

- **Expenses.** Will your assistant have to shell out any of their own money for you? Will you reimburse them? Normally, you can ask that any expenses be approved prior to purchase so that you can budget for them. You don't want any surprises!
- **Taxes.** You may want to make sure your contractor understands that they are responsible for paying their own taxes *unless* you have decided to get into an employee relationship with them, in which case you are responsible for paying the taxes. Either way, it's helpful for everyone to spell this out.
- **No Other Compensation.** This means that the payment you've expressed in this section is all that the assistant is getting. There are no benefits or bonuses that you've agreed upon.

(You can always give a bonus at any point for a job well done, you're just not promising anything here in the agreement.)

Nature of Relationship

Again, because you most likely have a contractor/1099 relationship on your hands, you want to be extra clear about what that means.

It's not a joint venture, a partnership, or an employer/ employee relationship. You are not responsible for paying taxes on behalf of the assistant and the assistant cannot set claim against you for health benefits, retirement, social security, workers comp, unemployment, or really any employee benefits of any kind. (Although when I started as a VA, all of this would have been nice!)

You are not liable for anything your assistant does in misrepresenting himself or herself, and your assistant is not beholden to you.

Contracts are all about protection. A misunderstanding about the nature of the relationship is one of those things you want to avoid.

Confidential Information and Non-Compete

Some people use a non-disclosure agreement as a supplemental bit of paperwork when working with new people and some use a confidential information clause in the contract. We will sign non-disclosures from clients on behalf of our entire company and team, but we put confidential information clauses and non-compete language in our contracts for assistants.

What does this mean? Well, you get to set your own terms here. For some, there aren't really any "trade secrets" or risk of spreading proprietary information. For others, sensitive, private, or innovative ideas are sacred and should certainly not be shared while the assistant is working with the company and for a period beyond the time they end their relationship.

At Don't Panic, our concerns are not so much with processes and systems as they are with private client information. Plus, and this is not something I like to think about, but it happens: We don't want the client/assistant relationships that we have matched to exist outside of our company. Essentially, we don't want clients to poach our assistants and we don't want our assistants to leave us to go work exclusively for a client.

Confidentiality clauses, non-competes, and non-solicitation agreements in both our client contracts and our assistant contracts help prevent that. You are not allowed to share confidential information or go work for one of our clients exclusively for a period of two years after working with us. We believe this is enough time for people to be dissuaded, forget, or simply move on.

Term & Termination

How long does this agreement last? Forever and ever into infinity and beyond? For a period of one year, at which point evaluation will occur?

And what happens if you run out of money or your assistant screws up?

In order to protect yourself and your investment, this section must be fair, yet conservative. You can't predict the future, so while you may be thinking, "I never want to terminate my assistant!", you just never know.

Most employment agreements stipulate a two-week notice, provided the employee didn't do anything illegal as grounds for being let go. In many contractor relationships, there's no specified notice and they can be let go for no reason or for a good reason, but not for a bad reason. This is similar to an employee-at-will agreement.

While you are not required to provide notice in a contractor relationship, it's not very nice not to. And in the spirit of positive work, I believe in being a reasonable boss/client. Treat your team how you wish to be treated. Provide notice so your assistant doesn't go hungry. That means making sure you're building in the budget to pay them for two weeks (or whatever) in the event that you need or want to let them go.

I've been in the horrible situation (only once, so far) where the client signed an agreement, started work, and proceeded to never pay his invoices. We had signed a similar agreement with an assistant for this client, so we were paying her regardless.

In our contracts, we charge a 10 percent late fee for invoices that are not paid after 30 days and we stop work if a client doesn't pay after 60 days. Well, that doesn't protect us from paying our assistants, and it's a risk we take each time we sign on with a new client.

When we hit the 60-day mark and couldn't get a hold of this client to get the payment he owed us for services, we gave his assistant her 14-day notice and ended his contract. If you're doing the math with me here, that's right, we essentially paid an assistant her full rate for two and a half months without getting a dime from this client.

(Can I say asshole? Because this client was a total asshole.)

This sort of situation isn't common, of course. If I was always doing business like this, I'd be bankrupt. But for us, a contract is binding and we honor binding contracts, unlike some other folks out there. This is also why having a cash reserve is so important. While I hope you never have to have any sort of experience like this, you need to protect yourself from worst-case-scenario situations.

Bonus: Vacation and Time Off

Since you're not an employer, you aren't required to provide any kind of vacation time or paid time off. But your assistant may want to protect their life and their schedule in some ways, so it's worth discussing a plan for what will happen if they want to spend a week in the Caribbean.

At Don't Panic, because we are a hybrid agency, we have a few days throughout the year that we are "closed," similar to traditional businesses. Memorial Day, Labor

Day, 4th of July, Thanksgiving, and the week between Christmas and New Year's Day are standard, but when we first started, we encountered a situation where a client was like, "Oh no, Bruno!"

You see, this client wanted to take the week off between Christmas and New Year's. And her inbox couldn't possibly be left alone for five days at the end of the calendar year.

Her assistant kindly brought this to my attention because she didn't know how to handle it. Should she say no, that our team was going to be needing a break, too? Should she suck it up and work over the holiday so that we wouldn't risk losing the client for the sake of a few days off? Should she find some sort of combination approach that makes everyone happy?

The client's VA and I ended up working together to create a schedule where we would alternate days checking in. That way we could share the burden, no one felt too taken advantage, and the client got what she wanted.

At the time, we were much less rigid as a company than we are now. We would make exceptions all over the place. I think I was just too nice and didn't want to risk tarnishing my reputation because of a few days of easy work. It was no skin off my back in the one-off scenario. Of course, over time this approach doesn't scale, but you know this already.

We learned an important lesson from a management perspective, however. Always discuss vacation/time off policies with clients and always schedule any vacations as far in advance as possible.

We also learned not to work with a client who is physically incapable of letting their inbox go unmonitored for five days. They are much too self-important and egotistical to be a good fit for us!

Even if you don't have a written "policy" per se, you still need to communicate about how you will handle the times when your assistant wants a few days off as well as what happens when you, as the client, want to go on vacation.

What things need to be checked? Should emails be forwarded somewhere? What constitutes an emergency? When should your assistant send a smoke signal and grab that margarita glass from your hand?

I added this second as a "bonus" because it's not necessarily something you need to include in a formal agreement, but it is something that's worth discussing around the same time that you're negotiating your contract because it could be related to payment.

Will your assistant still get paid if they take some time off? What about if you take time off? Most people will work in advance as much as possible so that they are still putting in the same amount of hours and should be paid as such. With an agency, you'll be provided with a backup assistant when there's a vacation so nothing gets lost. But when you go on vacation, you should either provide a list of tasks that can be done in your absence or plan to simply pay the normal retainer if you want to not keep a positive relationship with your VA. An assistant's paycheck shouldn't suffer just because you felt like hitting the slopes or hopping on a Mediterranean cruise.

Again, please consult with a lawyer before you finalize any agreement, but I hope these few must-haves will make it into your contracts.

If you need a nudge in the right direction, I've provided a template you can use for your virtual assistant agreements in Appendix I at the end of the book. There's also a link to download the Word doc version that you can manipulate for your own use. Because I'm nice like that.

Rule #3:

DON'T DRIVE THE BUS, CO-PILOT THE PLANE

chapter eleven

PUT THE "ME" IN TEAM

I recently finished reading *Good to Great* by Jim Collins. It's a worthwhile read for anyone in business and I can't believe it took me so long to finally finish it . . . I think my dad gave it to me as a high school graduation gift! Sorry, Dad.

In the book, Collins talks about getting the right people on the bus. It's more about the characteristics of these people than anything else. While you're driving the bus, your team is filling the seats behind you, chugging away at their jobs as you're on the road together.

I love this analogy and the supporting examples that Collins provides because they prove what I've always felt in my heart: soft skills are more important than hard skills in many business environments. And what's most important is that you're on the same road, the same path to success.

In a virtual assistant relationship, the sentiment is slightly different. Instead of you, the client, as the driver of a bus, consider another moving vehicle: an airplane. You and your assistant are both in the cockpit. You're going the same place, but you need each other to get there. You're the pilot, so you've got slightly more control, but your VA is your co-pilot and you need their help to navigate the skies.

This idea reminds me of another great book I finished recently, *The Checklist Manifesto* by Atul Gawande. Gawande is a surgeon and has spent years examining why things go wrong in the operating room. Through years of observation and research, he found that providing a simple checklist can make all the difference. He began examining this idea as a result of the success that pilots had with lists that both pilot and co-pilot would be required to follow in the event of an emergency.

While we're not performing surgery or actually flying a plane, a lot can be learned from *Good to Great* and *The Checklist Manifesto*: getting the right people in your corner is important, but making sure you're all on the same page about what needs to be done and when is paramount.

You need to make sure that you're working in tandem with your VA, both picking up the ball, both following the task list, and both communicating effectively and consistently to be successful.

This all starts with you.

So, first of all, congratulations! You've done half the work.

You've identified who you are, what you need, and you've gone to great lengths to find someone that suits you. That process often takes years for people because it's a mindset shift from, "I've got this all by myself!" to, "Holy shit I'm drowning and I need help RIGHT MEOW!"

Kudos to you for making the leap from not just thinking about getting help to actually finding help. Yay.

Now, the last thing you want to do is screw that all up like Fox did when they aired the first episodes of *Firefly* in the wrong order, failed to build a strong following as a result, and canceled the show, much to the dismay of loyal Joss Whedon fans worldwide. A real travesty that was. Don't be like Fox.

Instead, the next step is to set yourself up with a solid foundation from which to build a life-long relationship.

I want to tell you two stories: One about a major success and one about an epic failure. You'll be able to see clearly which was which, but at the time we started work, I could have argued that both of these client situations looked the same on paper.

That's what makes life difficult. You may have the exact same business model, the exact same challenges, and hire the exact same assistant (which is what happened here) but have a completely different outcome.

Why? Because of you. You set the tone for the relationship. You drive its success. Without "me," there is no team. You need to take that role seriously and I'll help show you how. But first . . . storytime!

Scenario #1: Courtney, CEO of a new public relations and communications agency.
Scenario #2: Deirdre, CEO of a new public relations and communications agency.

(See what I mean? Literally the same setup on paper. I chose these examples on purpose.)

The Situation

Courtney is the CEO of a growing public relations firm that she started after leaving her big agency job behind. (Note: Courtney is not her real name. You'll see why . . . Spoiler alert!) She wanted the flexibility of being the boss of her own business and had the experience in the industry to secure her own clients.

She was quickly able to support herself with a few big clients and found that the day-to-day tasks of invoicing, managing her inbox, and organizing her growing travel needs were not being taken care of because they took away from the time she needed to service clients. Like Don't Panic, Courtney put her clients' priorities first!

She knew it was time to get some help.

The Challenges

Before hiring Don't Panic, Courtney had never managed anyone before. She was a hard worker and earned a position at a large agency, but was still mostly in implementation mode, had her own clients, and wasn't too focused on anything but the happiness of those clients.

This is great because we always believe clients come first, but it can be tough to transition from working in an agency to going fully virtual in a new business on your own.

Her processes were, dare I say, nonexistent. The business was brand new, so this was understandable. Her lack of documented processes was part of why she wanted to hire someone who had a different brain than hers. While she focused on strategy and business development, she needed a detail-oriented and deadline-driven assistant to compile and manage the rest.

The Way Don't Panic Helped

In addition to getting her project management tool set up right away (we do love a good project management system!), we also organized her calendar and took over all scheduling duties immediately. She trained us on which coffee shops were the best ones to have meetings at and guided us on how many minutes she wanted to set aside for meetings with each type of contact.

Soon, we were not only sending invoices and handling the schedule for her personally, we also stepped into some client-facing projects. From research to social media management, we were able to grow our retainer with Courtney and she was able to back-fill some of her services with a part-time assistant instead of taking the leap to hiring someone full-time (which she knew she wanted to do, but wasn't ready for).

The Demise

Okay, so I was hoping to let this play out a little longer before giving away the secret, but rehashing all the details of what went on isn't necessary. This was the one that didn't work out. But it wasn't for lack of trying.

There were a number of things that started getting a little wacky, and though it started slow, an implosion was imminent so we were lucky to get out before that happened.

First, it was the use of the project management tool, or lack thereof. My advice to clients who are considering using a project management tool is always this: If you're going to use it, you have to use it 100 percent of the time. You can't have some things in your email, some things in the project management tool, some things in other tools, etc. And if you're not committed to putting everything into the tool yourself, you have to explain that to your assistant and ask them to do it for you.

Well, that wasn't going to happen. Comments, feedback, deadlines, and important messages were flying every which way. We were spending more time trying to compile each bit of information in one place than we had hours in the week, which meant that other tasks were falling by the wayside. This was the beginning of the end.

Next was that lovely old "entrepreneurial spirit" that had Courtney working near 14-hour days every day. When you start at 6 a.m. and something you requested isn't done by 12 p.m., it can feel like an eternity. I get that. But as you now well know, a virtual assistant isn't working for you 24-7, and you can never expect a six-hour turnaround time unless you've previously discussed and agreed upon it with your assistant.

Unrealistic expectations turned into animosity. She couldn't understand why we weren't working at her speed and we couldn't understand where that expectation came from.

We addressed the issue quickly, as we always aim to do with open communication, and the issue subsided.

For a time ...

Then it came back with a vengeance. Like that one grey hair you pluck and then it grows back twice as thick.

We decided to transition this client from one assistant to another, and it went well internally. Tasks were not lost and processes were well-documented. It was difficult to convince her that a new assistant was needed, but we wanted to see if we were the problem in this relationship. It was completely possible! After all, at Don't Panic, we always look inward at what we can change or fix or do better before we place any issue on the client.

The straw that broke the camel's back was a meeting with Courtney during which she complained that we weren't taking her projects seriously enough. She was also frustrated that this retainer was the only overhead her business had and why couldn't we respond faster to her requests?

Courtney was working with our minimum retainer, by the way, which is five hours per week. Five. Hours. Per. Week. That's about one hour per day. Which is just about enough to read emails, get a few small tasks done, and move on.

I wanted to grab her by the shoulders and shake her at this point. If you couldn't afford the services, why did you sign the contract? If you weren't clear about what you were getting, why didn't you ask?

This isn't brain surgery. This isn't rocket science. This is marketing, communications, and PR. No one is going to live or die.

The stress I felt from worrying about her all the time, getting weekend emails and after-hours text messages wasn't worth the meager retainer she was paying.

In the end, we realized that Courtney was not aware of her place in the world, not aware of how long things really take vs. how many hours she had in her contract, not respectful, and simply not kind. Her lack of planning led to our emergency day in and day out. And that wasn't fair.

This wasn't the sort of person we wanted to be working with or building our business with.

We suggested she may be better off hiring an intern or someone that she could micromanage in-house for a cheaper hourly rate.

She ended up hiring someone local that she could get more hours from. That was ultimately what she needed, and we were glad to pass off the opportunity to someone she could rely on for more.

The moral of this story?

Trial and error is inevitable, even necessary when you're working with new people. You don't need to have been a manager before or have processes in place before you pull the trigger.

What's most important is that you're open and honest in your communication, that you don't put the cart before the horse, that you're reasonable in what you're looking for (and that you're reflective about whether you were being honest with yourself about what you really needed), and perhaps above all, that you're not taking yourself too seriously.

I recently had my first experience with goat yoga. Yes, you heard that right. It's essentially a normal yoga class in terms of curriculum, but you're in a barn surrounded by baby goats. The goats make a lot of noise. They jump on your back and give you a little massage with their hooves while you're in tabletop or downward facing dog.

The best part about goat yoga is that it's impossible to beat yourself up about falling out of a pose, not being able to balance on one leg, or breathing like you just ran a marathon as opposed to that "gentle" breathing they are always rambling about. After all, you're surrounded by baby goats! Baby goats who go wherever they want and make the most ridiculous noises throughout the entire class.

I think everyone should go to goat yoga once in their life, just to experience this feeling of doing something really hard (yoga) while being distracted by something completely insane (baby goats). It makes you realize that nothing is so serious and no matter how hard we work, the goats don't care. They're going to cry out during the most quiet, peaceful moments and they're going to shit on you during the most perfect pose. And there's nothing you can do about it.

If that's not an analogy for life, I don't know what is. And by the way, I've heard this is very much what it's like when you're a work-at-home parent, so . . . well . . . sorry about that. Maybe you don't need to go to goat yoga if you're a WAHM or WAHD (work-at-home mom or dad) because you already get it. And I guess I have something to look forward to.

Anyway, Courtney realized she needed someone local as we realized we needed to get rid of her, so it ended up working out for everyone. She likes micromanaging, but it's impossible to do that from afar. She also needed someone to physically organize her life and we couldn't do that either.

When I think back to the unfortunate situation with Courtney, I want to tell her to try some goat yoga. Maybe make it a part of her weekly life. Because while

I do believe she learned a lot from our time together, I still think she, and many folks out there, are taking themselves and their businesses wayyyy too seriously. Because there's a difference between working hard and killing yourself (and the people around you) to make your business happen. And the latter never works for anyone in the long run.

Now, let's take a look at another story that ended a bit differently.

The Situation

Deirdre is the CEO of a growing communications agency, a college professor, an author, and the host of a popular podcast that streams worldwide. (Deirdre IS her real name. Hi, Deirdre! Big hugs!)

She stays busy, if that wasn't obvious already!

Deirdre came to Don't Panic Management because she was transitioning her business to a new model. She hoped this change would give her a bit more freedom than the constraints of agency life. She thought she'd have more time and that her workload would get lighter. Instead, she found the opposite to be true.

All the nitty gritty details of running a business were bogging her down and she couldn't ignore the nagging feeling that it was time to get some help.

Her biggest pain points were calendar organization and managing the increasing speaking and teaching opportunities that were coming her way. The growth she was experiencing was a great problem to have, but it was still a problem—she had more requests to field than she had working hours.

"My business has a lot of moving parts. I really need help managing my calendar and coordinating my event participation," she told us.

My team and I worked through several meetings and phone calls to understand her goals, clear her plate of immediate administrative tasks, and set up a proactive weekly cadence for managing her schedule. Soon, we were able to uncover some other areas of her business that we could help with as well.

The Challenges

Before working with Don't Panic, Deirdre was transitioning from an agency owner to a communications consulting business. She followed her passion for helping businesses become better communicators, but that also meant leaving many of the agency benefits behind—like working with an office manager and a dedicated assistant.

She had never worked with a virtual assistant before and was wary of how it would work for her when she was used to having people in the office with her.

"My main goal [in hiring Don't Panic] was to have a trusted resource manage and coordinate my daily calendar and interact with clients and event coordinators so I could focus on my book writing, interviews, speaking, and growing my business."

The Way Don't Panic Helped

It was obvious: Deirdre simply needed another set of eyes and ears on the ground to sort through her inbox, act as a liaison with her contacts, and keep her calendar organized. A Watson to her Sherlock.

Luckily, these are things that a trained assistant is able to take on very easily with a bit of guidance.

As our working relationship evolved over the weeks and months, so did Deirdre's goals. With the extra hours back in her day, she was able to focus more time on developing her podcast. When it got to the point where she didn't have the resources to build the podcast out any further without some outside help, we were able to step in.

"We're now focused more on the podcast, which is an important part of my brand and business. Don't Panic Management has moved beyond just providing a VA for my daily calendar into having her coordinate all of my interviews and interact with publicists. I also use the team for podcasting production. The increase in work and the goals are evolving together."

Evolving together! Getting shit done! That's what the Don't Panic Management team is all about.

The Don't Panic Proven Process

Don't Panic has found that the best way to build a personalized, long-lasting relationship with our clients is through meticulous matchmaking and ongoing evaluation. Deirdre is a prime example of a client that has worked with multiple Don't Panic Management assistants throughout her time with us but hasn't had to "start over" each time.

It can be difficult when you've invested months and sometimes years into developing a relationship with an assistant, only to get word that they've found another job. With a typical freelancer or employee, you'd be left back at square one. But with Don't Panic, Deirdre's first assistant had set up written processes based on Deirdre's requests that made transitioning from one assistant to another as simple as a few hours of internal training and a quick introduction meeting with Deirdre.

She didn't have to invest more time into training this new person because the handoff between team members was all done for her behind the scenes.

We've incorporated a variety of services into her contract over the years as her needs have grown and changed (like any healthy relationship does!). For nearly six months, we managed her company's social media platforms. After that time, Deirdre evaluated the process and felt that some of her internal team members were actually doing the same work that we were doing, so it would be easier and more streamlined to bring that work in-house. We were happy to work with her team to offload the work product and processes we'd been handling on so that her business's social channels didn't skip a beat.

It's such a blast working with Deirdre because she's flexible enough to try new things, but also knows what works best for her business. Some of the services we've tried needed to be handled internally, and that's okay. Other services were best outsourced to my team.

It's our goal to serve without ego. And that means jumping in to help wherever we fit best and letting go of the rest.

The Result & ROI

Currently, Don't Panic Management assists Deirdre with Virtual Administrative Support and Podcast Production. We've been working together since early 2015. In that time, Deirdre's been able to write another book to add to her repertoire, grow her business by at least 30 percent, participate in developing three LinkedIn Learning video courses (with more to come in the future), and has hosted the NASDAQ #PRInfluencers panel discussion series live in New York City, among many other achievements.

In our conversations, Deirdre shared with us that she has been 100 percent satisfied in what we've done to help her meet her goals and explains that the ROI of working with Don't Panic has made her more relaxed, both personally and professionally.

"There is no need to panic; I know my VA has my back," she says. "I've also seen an increase in business and speaking opportunities as a result of my ability to focus more on these areas. I was able to write and work with my publisher to gear up for a new book launch. My VA was instrumental in keeping me organized during a very busy time."

When asked if there was anything she'd change about working with Don't Panic, Deirdre said, "I don't want anything to change. I appreciate the level of accountability and communication you provide. I feel comfortable moving through the crazy highs and sometimes lows of business with you, knowing we're a team working toward the same goals."

The Future

We're currently in talks to work on podcasting recording support for live events with Deirdre, which we're super excited about. Deirdre said it best on a recent episode of her podcast (that features yours truly):

"I do believe that what you put into it is what you're going to get out of it. It's a relationship. When you talk about building trust with any assistant, whether it's a physical person who follows you around or a virtual assistant, *you're the other half of that relationship.* You have to determine how much you want to give so that person on the receiving line can actually grow with you and you can do great things together, and they can be an even better resource for you."

She took the time to build that relationship with us up front, she communicated her preferences in detail, and she helped us set up systems that have allowed us to make her time spent working more efficient. That means she has more of it to lead a purposeful, independent life.

Now, that's something to celebrate!

I swear, you guys, I didn't ask for her to say that. She said it all on her own. But with almost three years of working together, she has earned this. She told us what she wanted out of our relationship and we worked hard together to make that happen for her.

I share this model client/assistant relationship because it sparks the ideas and values that I hope will pervade the virtual work space:

- Treat your assistant how you would want to be treated.
- Spend the time training and getting to know your assistant if you want them to be a rock star for your business.
- Ask and you shall receive.

It's that simple, folks.

You're the secret ingredient in determining whether any relationship can possibly be a success. That's why putting the "me" in "team" is so valuable.

chapter twelve

WHATEVER YOU DO, DON'T BE A SHITTY CLIENT

I hope you put your grown-up pants on today because we're about to use some adult language. And if you've been reading this book aloud to your children, now is a good time to stop. Ha, I know you're not reading this book to anyone except maybe yourself. But next on my book release schedule is . . . a children's book! So get excited about that.

Just kidding.

To get back to the point, there's a reason this site exists: https://clientsfromhell.net

It's a catalog of stories from freelancers who have dealt with the most heinous of situations as they try, desperately, to get their projects done. And it only reinforces a sentiment I've known as long as I've been in business:

Most people are terrible at being clients.

It makes sense. It's not anyone's fault. Nobody teaches you how to be a good client in school. Perhaps you've never *been* anyone's client before. Or you've worked for clients in the past but the same courtesies you expect from those clients don't apply to you when you're a client.

Whatever the explanation, it's time to stop it with the Shitty Client Syndrome. Why? A few reasons:

1. When You're a Shitty Client, No One Wants to Help You

In the digital age, news travels fast. You've seen it with the Kardashian Snapchat photos and the neverending drama between one celebrity split and another. The internet makes the world a smaller place and people are communicating more than ever (even if that communication is via emails, texts, and direct messages as opposed to real life conversations!).

When you treat a freelancer or agency or assistant unfairly or you're mean or you don't pay your bills on time, people talk about it. Our industry is not that big. Do you want a referral for a great VA? VAs want good referrals for the clients they choose to take on, too.

We'll ask around, especially if a client was sent to us by someone we know.

We'll see if you have worked with a VA before and find out what happened during the course of the relationship. We'll ask how you pay and when. We'll also ask some more general questions about how you work to try and gauge whether or not you have a good workflow set up. We'll attempt to determine how you're going to treat us.

There are two sides to every story. We understand that. But if we hear from more than one person that you're not fun to work with, you'll have a hard time getting great people to work with you.

2. When You're a Shitty Client, You Get a Shitty Result

If you've gotten this far and you're going through one assistant after the other with little consequence (except for the fact that you have to reinvent the wheel every time), you probably won't be able to find *another* great person to help you. That means you'll end up with a shitty person. And shitty people provide shitty work.

3. When You're a Shitty Client, You're Miserable (And So Is Everyone Else)

When you're constantly providing things at the last minute, changing your mind all the time, and only ever giving negative feedback (plus the obvious, just being a jerk and not making payments on time) you make yourself and everyone else around you very sad.

Who wants to be sad?

No one, that's who.

Let's go over a few ways to not be a shitty client. Hopefully this doesn't apply to you. But it might and you might not realize it. That's called not being self-aware. Come on. Go back to chapter 2. I'll wait.

. . .

Ready? Here are 11 things you can do right now to be a better client and earn a better outcome from your VA. Even if you only adopt a few of these, your assistant will notice and may decide to continue working with you. I said MAY. You're walking on thin ice if you're doing the opposite of what I tell you here. Remember, if a VA can get the same amount of hours and dollars from someone else who is nicer to them, they will.

1. Know What You Want

Do not, I repeat, do not hire a virtual assistant and then say, "Okay, what can you do for me?"

Sure, it's fine to not be sure of exactly what you're looking for during the scouting and hiring process. Many times, once you find someone you like and you determine their skill set, you can decide which things you want to delegate to them.

But that's BEFORE you become a client. Not after you sign the contract.

You have to go in order here. Follow the process in Chapter 2 for becoming aware of your loves so you can delegate the rest. Take your time with this. And ideally, you'll be able to follow this process time and time again as you grow with your assistant because, inevitably, your loves and needs will change.

(I recommend revisiting your list once a year, at the very least. Around the new year makes sense, but you can do it whenever you find yourself getting itchy for the next thing.)

Change is okay. Unplanned change is not. VAs thrive on making your world go around, but they can't do that if you're constantly changing your mind about what you want them to do.

2. Get Yourself Organized

There's a common desire I hear from people I talk to in new business meetings. They say, "I am the big ideas person and I need someone to be the implementer." Okay, that's great, you're onto something here and you've come to the right place.

But when I ask people to organize the tasks and projects they need to get off their plate and they say, "No Jess, I'm disorganized. That's WHY I need a VA!"

To which I say, "STOP MAKING EXCUSES!"

I know that not everyone is naturally a Type A neat freak, but becoming organized doesn't have to be a born trait. It can be a learned skill that you can practice over time.

Take it from me. My nickname growing up (at least in kindergarten) was Messy Jessy. I left a train wreck of toys and clothes and food and everything in between anywhere I went. Even still, I can't always get myself to put my laundry away or get the dishes into the dishwasher. My fiancé likes to refer to me as a Tasmanian Devil, leaving a trail of destruction in my wake everywhere I go.

So yes, I am not naturally an organized person.

But when it came to work, I knew I needed to get my shit together so I could actually, you know, get anything done.

Now, while I'm not a model for perfect organizational skills, I know what being organized looks like in action. Just like anything else, your process for organizing your work and your life can be your own. There at least needs to be some semblance of it, otherwise how are you going to be able to give someone access to your life?

If you're not interested in actually being organized, you can pretend. Over time, pretending to be organized will help you see what it's like to actually be organized and then you can reevaluate your stubbornness about how organization can change your life. (I'm speaking from experience.) Here are a few very easy ways you can pretend to be organized:

1. Go through all the files you use frequently or need to keep around. Put those files in folders in Dropbox or Drive and label those folders according to what the contents are. ALWAYS put files in folders and don't let any stragglers get away. Or ask your assistant to organize these files for you, but make sure you tell them HOW you want them to be organized. Then, either always give new files to the assistant to organize or file them away yourself.

2. Make to-do lists every day, week, and month of all the things you need to and/or want to get done. If for no other reason, do this because the satisfaction of crossing something off as done on your to-do list is like sliding your hand into a big bag full of dry beans and squishing them. Am I the only one that loves to do that? Oh well. To-do lists are great for seeing progress, organizing your brain about what's truly important, and setting and achieving goals to make you feel like the badass you are. Bonus: Give yourself a reward when you reach a certain goal or cross off a certain number of tasks. A cookie, a fresh cup of coffee, a new pair of shoes. See? Organizing can be fun!

3. Remove clutter. Keep your work space physically and emotionally clear of random pieces of paper, mail, pens, half-eaten snacks, and glasses. Go to the goddamn Container Store! That place allows you to buy a container for everything so you can, you know, put things away. I recommend cleaning up your workspace (and your mental space) at the end of every day so you arrive the next morning with a fresh space, or you can also do it in the morning

before you start to work. No matter when you do it, make sure you are, in fact, doing it.

4.   Write everything down. The busier you get, the less space you'll have in your brain to remember everything. When I was first starting my work as a VA, I had two clients. I could literally wake up in the morning and know exactly what I had to do that day, when, and for whom. Now? It's like a war zone up there. Remembering everything from birthdays to speaking application due dates to employee reviews is just too much. I prefer to use a physical notebook for writing down my thoughts, reminders, and tasks, but I also use my phone to remind me of things like this: "Hey Siri, remind me to pick up my prescription tomorrow at 10 a.m." She'll set a reminder in my phone and tell me how to get to the pharmacy in case I forget. (It's happened before.) I also use our team's project management tool when my tasks rely on or are followed by other people's tasks. I've learned (the hard way) that the more I can get out of my head and onto the page, whether it's a digital or analog page, the more space I have for higher level thinking and creating. Why waste your precious memory on anything other than things you must remember, like childhood play dates, spousal preferences, and the right amount of parmesan to add to the frittata. (Although, to be fair, you can write those down too! It just might be embarrassing if you have to go refer to your diary or something to recall a fun trip to Disney World with your family. Also, the right amount of parmesan to put on anything is all of it.)

A lack of organization wastes your time. Perhaps more importantly at this point, it wastes other people's time. And if you're paying for other people's time, you don't want it to be wasted trying to find a file or a rogue calendar appointment, do you?

I mentioned this before and I'll mention it again: Go read Marie Kondo's *The Life-Changing Magic of Tidying Up* if you're getting the organizational high right now. Then go KonMari the shit out of your life.

3. Set Up Clear Outcomes and (Reasonable) Deadlines

When you're working in a contractor relationship, you can't really tell someone HOW you want something done. The way they work is technically up to them. But you can tell them what you want and when you want it. So do that.

Give them your goals for a project. Tell them you want to see a spreadsheet of all the podcasts that would be a good fit for you given that your topics are X and Y. Tell them you want to make sure they include the podcast name, host name, website URL, iTunes URL, Twitter account, and contact email address if they can find it. Tell them you want at least 20 podcasts by end of day next Friday. Let them run wild.

The way they go about finding those podcasts is up to them. (You can, of course, give them some hints, like if you've been hoarding top 10 lists of podcasts for months hoping to do this project yourself, then send them that list.) And you can offer support along the way. For example, if this is a new person and you don't want them to waste anybody's time, ask for a list of ten that you can review to start with and then let them know, quickly, whether or not they're on the right track.

Don't be vague. Don't beat around the bush with what you really want. If you do, you'll end up in a situation where your VA thought you wanted 15 different social media templates but really you wanted call-to-action buttons for your website.

Sharing the goal may not seem important at the time, and maybe it's not for that particular project, but keeping goals front and center certainly never hurts. (Unless it's some sort of confidential spy project that you'll get killed for if you share it. In that case, maybe don't hire a VA to help you with it . . .)

As usual, this takes work on your part. You need to be clear about what it is that you really want and why you want it before you can make an assignment for your assistant.

4. Don't Change Your Mind (Unless You MUST)

If there's one thing I know about virtual assistants, it's that they like reliability. Yes, they can be flexible if needed, and the best assistants will bend to your needs because they have the skills to pivot on a dime. Starting a project, getting into a groove, and generating results only to be told to stop and start over again because you had a change of heart is not only inefficient, it's frustrating and impacts morale in a negative way.

Sometimes changes happen and they're out of your control. A budget was adjusted or a timeline was pushed up or an initial goal wasn't as set in stone as you planned.

We understand these things happen. The best thing to do in these situations is, first, obviously, avoid them by planning everything in advance. If they can't be avoided, communicate the change as early as humanly possible. Be honest about what happened and why. Sometimes people just need to understand the reason and then they can move forward without worrying too much about their wasted effort.

Also, remember that any changes in scope may result in a change in timeline, so don't expect everything to get done on time if you've changed even one piece of the puzzle.

I once had a client who hired my team to help with one of his own client projects. We do this often, backfilling services for other agencies that want to expand their offerings without expanding their team. In this case, my client was focused on the production side of marketing and he was looking for a social media and email support team to execute the strategic marketing plan he had created for his client.

When it turned out that his client (this is the client of my client, which is annoyingly confusing, I know) actually needed a website overhaul before any of the marketing plans could effectively begin, we were left with a complete scope change that we couldn't handle ourselves. After all, we are an administrative and marketing support team, not a website design and development team.

Luckily, I was able to call a friend and colleague to pinch hit and provide a consultation and, ultimately, a website that met the client's desires. But even that project was a total train wreck because they kept changing their minds about what should go where and how it should all function.

Since they were unclear about their goals and outcomes, everyone around them—who, by the way, were trying their darnedest to make them happy as clams—was forced to scramble, cut corners, re-do work again and again, and ultimately lose money, faith, and patience throughout the process.

In hindsight, I should have seen the warning signs sooner than I did and ended the relationship before it got too out of control. The pleaser in me really wanted to help them be successful. The reality is that some people, even if they read this book right now, will never change. Sigh.

Anywho, assuming you're not that sort of client, all I ask is that after communicating the change and its details to the appropriate parties, check in with your assistant, pretty please. See if they can even handle the kind of change you're talking about or if you're going to need to hire outside support. Also, assuming they can handle whatever change you've made, make sure to ask if this is going to affect their delivery plans.

You can push for a certain goal but you can't force a deadline after you made a significant change unless you're either taking something else off their plate or adding a few days/weeks to the timeline.

5. Check Your Attitude

Virtual relationships naturally involve a layer of uncertainty. You know how you can't see me working in my PJs? I also can't see if you woke up on the wrong side of the bed.

In an office environment, an assistant may be able to sense that you're in a bad mood one day and offer to grab your coffee for you or hold the door. They may be extra cautious with asking you for things or putting too much on your plate.

In a virtual environment, we unfortunately cannot witness those things as easily. And even if we could, it's not our job to make you feel better all the time.

Leave your baggage at home. Or better yet, air it out through some meditation or therapy or yelling into a pillow. Don't bring it into the professional working environment.

If you do find yourself stuck with a bad attitude one day and you know it's affecting your communication with your team, maybe just tell everyone, "Hey, I'm pissed off because my mother-in-law has been staying at my house for three weeks now, and they're doing construction on the bathroom so we all have to share one, small half-bath and I can't find a way to get my dog to stop chewing on the carpet."

You may feel nervous about being an honest human, but I can guarantee that by sharing your *mood*, whatever it may be, you'll feel a weight lifted off your chest and your team will breathe a sigh of relief. Instead of thinking they were the ones who were causing you angst, everyone can stop tiptoeing around you and move on.

6. Provide Ongoing, Timely, Consolidated Feedback

No one likes to go into a review meeting dreading the worst because they have no idea what you're thinking. An assistant should never not know how they're doing and should never be told only at the very end of a project how it went.

As the client and the manager, it's your job to stay on top of the work that they're doing and to make sure it's going well day in and day out.

I'm not saying you have to be checking and double checking everything your VA does every second of every day. That would be a whole job in and of itself! Part of the benefit of hiring a virtual assistant is that they have the skills and experience and wherewithal to know how to do something well without being coddled along the way. In order to avoid passive-aggressive texts, mismanaged expectations, and a disgruntled assistant, give clear, timely feedback all the time. Don't wait until something goes wrong. Make it a habit to always respond with, "Thanks, great job!" Or, "This looks good, but if you could add this one piece of information it would be amazing!" Or, "I thought I had asked for delivery in this format, but you sent it to me in that format. Can you please re-format and send? Thank you!"

Every interaction is an opportunity for feedback and the more you tell your assistant what you do and do not like, the sooner they can start providing things in a way that makes you happy.

Just like with sex . . . oh okay, now we're getting somewhere! Just kidding. I know an assistant relationship isn't the same as a spousal one, as we've discussed, but you get where I'm going with this.

Now, one thing that you may need to work on (most of us do) is providing feedback in a consolidated fashion. So, for example, don't start reviewing a project and hitting send on an email for every piece of feedback you have. I once had a client who was constantly doing this and then wondering why we may have missed a piece of feedback. IT'S BECAUSE YOU SENT NINETY-FIVE SEPARATE EMAILS ABOUT IT AND MY INBOX THOUGHT YOU WERE A SPAM BOT.

Instead, take notes on the project as you go. You can write them in the body of an email if you want or in your project management tool. Just do NOT send the email until you've gone through the entire project, thought about it a little bit more, and maybe even have gone through it all again.

Your goal with feedback is to have your assistant make positive changes and to only have to provide the same feedback once. If your assistant has to spend time deciphering what you're trying to say and parsing through tons of notes in different places or different threads, you're guaranteed to get a mediocre result at best.

7. Remember That Your Assistant Will Never Care As Much As You Do

I once had a client who was truly egotistical. He thought he walked on clouds and all the work he did at his agency deserved the highest awards.

He had hired me for five hours per week to help with some administrative tasks as well as some project management work on client projects that he didn't have time for. He happened to fit into a lot of the "shitty client" categories (changed his mind all the time, had poor communication skills, nickel-and-dimed, was always in a bad mood) but one of the biggest hurdles that we could never seem to overcome was his unspoken desire for me to be his partner in business.

Deep down, I don't think he was ready to start his own business in the first place and that's why he needed so much help. But he couldn't understand why, again, with only five hours a week, I wasn't making business development recommendations or volunteering to help with client relationships given all of my knowledge running a client-based services business.

Sure, I was growing my own business as well with success and perhaps he wanted to utilize the ideas that worked for me.

Over and over I found myself wanting to grab him by the shoulders and say, "Hey dude! This isn't what you hired me for!"

If you want strategic coaching, leadership advice, or sales and marketing consulting, there are plenty of people out there for that. Coaches, consultants, leadership advisors, or even your therapist can help in that department. (Can you tell how much I highly recommend every adult get the help of an awesome therapist?)

Unfortunately, a virtual assistant does not fall into that category (even though it does seem like VAs are lifesavers sometimes, just like coaches and therapists!).

This is a huge issue and can be a bit more difficult to recognize and wrap your head around, I think, because of course, your business is your baby and you want everyone to see it as something to cherish and grow as much as you do.

Even a coach or consultant won't ever care as much as you do (no matter what they say). It's not their baby, after all. It's yours.

8. Be Willing to Hear Another Point of View

Okay, so I just finished telling you that you shouldn't expect anything more than the work you hired for from your assistant. But! As you build trust and camaraderie over time, your assistant's experience and expertise may crop up in unexpected ways.

For example, you may be using the same tired, old project management tool that you started your business with five years ago. Perhaps you love it to pieces, but it's no longer being supported by the developers who created it and you're finding bugs left and right that you can't get anyone to help you solve.

Your VA has worked with other clients and has experience with lots of other project management tools. She suggests that perhaps you move off of the sad, dying, outdated piece of software and onto one that is newer, shinier, and just plain works better.

She even volunteers to train you on how to use the new tool and to help you make the painstaking transition so nothing gets lost.

Now, I won't lie here: oftentimes VAs make recommendations because they make their lives easier as well. They're sick of tasks disappearing or comments being sent to the wrong email address in a crappy project management tool, yes, but perhaps they also already have an account and a solid grasp of another tool that they can more seamlessly integrate with the workflow they have set up with their other clients.

While you must evaluate your assistant's recommendations personally and make sure they make sense for you, I don't think there's anything wrong with taking a piece of advice if it's the better fit for your needs and makes your VA's life easier. After all, if they're the ones using the tool, following the process, or checking the system, then shouldn't they at least be able to weigh in on what it looks like and how it works?

You should never blindly take a piece of advice or recommendation from someone else (except from me in this book, of course!), even if you trust them and have worked with them for a long time. You can, at the very least, be open and willing to listen to reasons, pros, and cons for anything that could potentially make your life easier and make your business grow.

9. Don't Nickel and Dime Your Team

"This is my only overhead cost, so I need every cent to count."

I've heard this sentiment more than once from small businesses that have gone out on a limb to hire my team. Maybe their friend or their coach has pushed them to hire a VA even though they didn't feel like they could afford it. Maybe they heard that even though my team is a little more expensive than other VAs, it's worth it because we have the exact experience and expertise they're looking for.

Some people I know have been taught to barter on everything. I can't figure out where this came from. One too many flea market experiences? A poor upbringing?

Look, if someone tells you their price, that's their price. If you do manage to negotiate down for whatever reason, you don't then get to remind them about it when things get hard.

I really don't understand why someone would hang a VA's cost over their head. Do people do that to you? Imagine if they did. How would you feel?

All VAs have are themselves. Their brains. Their own two hands. Pricing out their services is hard enough and, believe you me, they spend a painstaking amount of time figuring out exactly how much money they need to make to pay their bills. Then, if they're smart, they increase their prices every year or two to account for inflation and their own added experience and expertise. They also try to make their pricing fair and competitive with the market. If you don't like it, go find someone else who is more affordable.

Remember, there are tons of little VA fishies in the sea. It's a bigger, better marketplace than ever before. But whatever you choose, choose it with your whole heart. Don't go back on the cost. Don't complain about the cost. And never make your assistant feel like they're anything less than worth their price.

(Unless they suck. Then give them feedback and try to get them to succeed before letting them go and finding someone you like better. It happens.)

10. Be Respectful

Okay, okay. Everyone says this. And some people say you need get respect to give it. Or you need to earn it. Or some other bullshit.

I'm here to say this: Respect means a lot of different things to a lot of different people and it comes in many forms. Here are just a few:

Show up on time. So simple, so underrated. People are busy. You're busy. If you show up late to a meeting, or worse, MISS a meeting (the agony!) then someone else's time got wasted and now you have to pay to reschedule. It better be a very rare occasion for you to be late and it better be a huge deal for you to straight up miss an appointment. If you're not going to show this courtesy for yourself, then do it for whoever else is involved, whether it be a hairdresser or a podcast guest or a prospective client.

Use your words and be kind. This goes back to the attitude conversation but it's slightly different: Not being an asshole is one thing. Being genuinely kind is another. Notice what's going on in your assistant's life. Don't have a meltdown if they screw something up. Say something, provide the feedback, and use positive language and tone while doing it. That level of courtesy and respect goes a long way.

Pay your bills on time. I'm noticing a theme here! Time! There's nothing more disrespectful than working your ass off for someone and then not getting paid promptly for your services. Too busy to pay? Forget to pay? Set up a calendar alert. Set up an automatic payment system. Or, better yet, get your VA to pay your bills for you! Honestly, it's not weird. I've had plenty of clients for whom I've paid my own invoice (with permission). One of them even said, "Don't pay this until it's due," which was technically 30 days after I sent it. Fine, not a problem. Paying on time tells your VA that you value their services and that you want to keep working with them. It tells them that they matter and that you notice their work.

A little bit of respect goes a long way. Don't let your pride or your ego get in the way of treating your VA right.

11. Don't Freaking Panic

Just like Cher relies on Sonny to hit the right note on the harmony, so an assistant relies on his client to keep their shit together.

Things are going to go wrong. A blog post will get published automatically when you didn't want it to. A tweet will accidentally get sent during a crisis that was insensitive. A client will get called by the wrong name or be taken to the wrong address or dial-in number.

Mistakes happen. Oh, but good things happen, too! You get an influx of new business and it coincides with your assistant's calendar opening up and you're so excited because it means that you can double this month's revenue and pay off that nagging credit card bill.

It's a rollercoaster being a business owner. But you get to choose how you react to all of it.

Keep. Your. Shit. Together.

And if you can't, talk to someone. Get some help from someone. But don't let that someone be your assistant. You need to keep your authority as a leader. You need to show that you are the captain of this ship and that this ship is not going to sink.

Speaking of ships . . .

chapter thirteen

JUST KEEP SWIMMING

As a virtual assistant agency owner, it's my number one goal to not only find you a great VA, but to keep you happy forever and ever. I don't want you to ever have to look for another VA for as long as your business exists and I want you to have someone who grows and evolves with you.

That's because team turnover is extremely expensive. A study from the Center for American Progress[1], which cites eleven research papers published over a 15-year period, shows that the average cost of turning over an employee in a highly skilled role is 213% of their salary.

Now, the cost of turnover when you're working with part-time contractors may not be quite that high, but

---

1. Boushey, Heather, and Sarah Jane Glynn. "There Are Significant Business Costs to Replacing Employees." Center for American Progress, 16 Nov. 2012, www.americanprogress. org/issues/economy/reports/2012/11/16/44464/there-are-significant-business-costs-to-replacing-employees/.

it's much more economical to encourage our team members to stay, limit turnover, and avoid losing that sort of money.

Well, obviously we do it together, so don't think you're off the hook for even one minute! I know, I'm really making you work here, huh?

Ongoing success means ongoing communication, feedback, and support from both sides. I've seen too many folks do all the work to set their assistant up for success only to leave them alone in a lurch when things really start to get going.

In an ideal world, your assistant *will* be able to anticipate your needs, read your mind, and perform all the tasks you've ever needed with glowing accuracy and timeliness. That is what you want! But with VAs, you can never simply "set it and forget it." Just as with a marriage, VA relationships must be nurtured.

Say it with me: Virtual assistants are people. The autopilot feature on an airplane is a robot.

This shouldn't be a tedious, painful process. I mean, you should actually *like* your assistant after all so it should be a priority for you to be in regular communication with them. The more time you spend training, mentoring, and building the relationship, the more you're going to be able to get out of your assistant and the more you and your assistant will begin to care about each other.

The caring isn't something you can buy. But it is something you can earn.

I wanted to share a few strategies that you can implement once you've worked out some of the first month's kinks. In my experience, it takes at least three months to get into a good groove with your assistant, sometimes up to a year depending on how many hours per week you're working with them. These strategies can be implemented pretty quickly and I encourage you to keep using them even after you think you don't need to anymore.

1. Schedule Weekly Recurring Meetings

When you first start working with someone new, you're going to be talking to them all the time. Lots of modern tools have made this easier than ever, from messaging apps like Slack to the pervasive use of mobile phones. A quick text, email, or direct message when you're thinking about something or need to provide feedback is awesome.

But nothing replaces good old phone conversations, even if, and perhaps especially if, you have nothing urgent to talk about.

Ann Handley, who wrote the fabulous foreword to this book, has been working with me and Don't Panic since 2013. We started our weekly meetings then and have never stopped. The only reason we cancel or reschedule them is if one of us is literally on a plane, on stage, or on vacation. Even then, we often talk during vacations. Just to catch up. It makes her feel better while she's relaxing to have that touch point.

We always have an agenda of topics (or, should I say, I have the agenda of topics, because it's not her job to run the meeting!), and we always spend some time catching up. It goes something like this:

> **Jess:** "How are you?"
> **Ann:** "Doing well. I'm just a little overwhelmed!"
> **Jess:** "What's going on?"
> **Ann:** "Oh, just preparing for this speech and trying to figure out the best way to share this example." Or, "I hate overnight flights!" Or, "I need help prioritizing this project over that one." Or, "I need to find Hamilton tickets!!!" Or any number of other things that could be going on that week.
> **Jess:** "Let's talk about it!"

And so we spend five minutes talking through some of her "Annxieties" as we lovingly call them, and usually she feels better after venting to someone who understands most of what she's going through. (Because I booked those speeches or flights and have also purchased Broadway tickets in my life!)

Then, we talk about our dogs for another few minutes. It's just necessary for us. And then we get to my agenda.

I always share the following:

- Schedule notifications
- New calendar updates

- Requests for interviews, podcasts, appearances, speeches, bylines
- Travel that's coming up in the next two months
- Flights that have been or need to be booked
- Any other random requests or messages I don't know how to respond to
- Feedback on anything Ann needs, like research help or project management assistance

This usually lasts anywhere from five to twenty minutes depending on how frantic the week is. When you're a busy author, speaker, and executive, the summer and winter are slower and fall and spring are crazier. While we always set aside thirty minutes for these meetings, I generally keep the full hour open in case we need to go over, which does happen periodically during the busy seasons.

In addition to the obvious updates here, which are really important for Ann to know because she cannot possibly pay attention to every single email thread, we also get the chance to just talk. We talk about things Ann is worried about. We talk about weird inquiries that arrived in our inboxes. We talk about requests for Ann's time or upcoming plans.

While I still always run things by her, these weekly conversations have made me more comfortable with her style, her needs, and how her brain works. Week by week, month by month, year by year, I can almost pretty much read her mind, or at least predict how she would respond to something 95 percent of the time.

That didn't happen because I'm so amazing at being a VA. I mean I *am* so amazing (and humble, clearly). But being amazing or mediocre has nothing to do with the information and knowledge I gain from listening carefully and asking thoughtful questions on these weekly calls. They help me anticipate Ann's needs. They help Ann feel more secure about what's going on. And they help us both grow our relationship to the point where now we're like this:

This is @JessOstroff refusing to entertain me

(That's me asleep for MAYBE 30 minutes on a flight from Boston to San Francisco. And that's Ann sitting next to me, having the time of her life.)

When You Don't Need a Weekly Call

If you use an admin VA, you need a weekly call. Please trust me on this. Don't try to get out of it unless you're *really* slammed or traveling. Even in that case, I recommend rescheduling, not canceling. It's really important.

If you're not using a VA for administrative, timely tasks, you may not need a weekly call. For example, let's say you're using a VA for ghostwriting. You are super on the ball and provide a monthly assignment memo that includes article headlines, a paragraph description of what you're looking for, and a few takeaways. (You are my dream client, by the way. DO THIS!)

You probably do a lot of your communication with your VA via email because it's a matter of sharing files, writing comments, sending drafts back for revisions, and so on.

If you have a call on the books, even if it's only once or twice a month, you're really doing yourself a favor. This way, you're able to discuss the assignment memo and clarify any gaps in instruction. You're able to let your writerly VA inside your mind if you have topics you've been kicking around and you're able to learn more about what your VA enjoys writing about so you can receive higher quality pieces. I know all of these things sound very non-urgent, very fluffy, and very unnecessary (because who wants more meetings, right?). But over time, I promise you, they make a HUGE difference in the quality of the work and the health and longevity of the relationship.

2. Say What You Mean and Mean What You Say

Your relationship with your VA is meant to be sacred. You are trusting them with sensitive information that perhaps you've never shared with anyone else. I know, you can't just trust anyone blindly. Trust must be earned. But through your weekly meetings, your ongoing positive work product, and the tangible feeling of calm you'll begin to experience, the comfort level between you and your assistant will naturally grow.

As a result, you should feel safe telling your assistant how you're feeling, honestly. I said it earlier and I'll say it again: We are not there with you each morning so we can't tell whether or not you got up on the right side of the bed.

If you're nervous about something, if something urgent comes up, or if you're mad because your flight got moved and it's nobody's fault but you just need to vent, tell us! We can't always do anything for you, but we can at least listen. Sometimes a good ear is all you need.

One thing is for sure: we can never do a single thing about anything unless we know about it. So you have to tell us.

On the other side of the coin, have you ever heard of positive reinforcement? Like when you're trying to train your dog to lie down and you give him treats as soon as his belly hits the floor? VAs need that too.

A simple, quick email or text message will do the trick. A note that says, "Hey, I know you're really working hard on this project and I just want you to know I appreciate it," is enough. You don't need to do it all the time, we're not praise-hungry wolves over here. But if you ever find yourself feeling grateful, that's the time to say something.

A simple message of positive affirmation goes a very, very long way in sustaining a positive relationship with a VA. They can't live on negative, constructive feedback alone. Remember, VAs are generally pleasers. If they don't know whether or not they're pleasing you, they will feel lost.

If you're not good at words of affirmation (I will freely admit I am not), practice makes perfect. Oh hey, you can feel free to practice on me if you want!

A good rule of thumb is to give twice as much positive feedback as negative feedback. To learn more about providing feedback and being a great manager, I'll recommend Kim Scott again. Kim also has a podcast, which is helpful for quick snippets of useful info about how to manage your team.

3. Referrals Represent the Mother of Appreciation

There are other ways to show love to your VA besides simply saying nice things to them. For example, a referral. A referral is probably the most meaningful way to say to the world, "This person is so awesome that I am willing to risk my reputation to recommend them to you."

For me, referrals were how I was able to quit my horrible job. Referrals were what allowed me to search for my soul (and find it). Referrals were, and continue to be, how I have grown and doubled my business year in and year out.

Without the kindness and generosity of my clients' referrals, I'm not sure where I'd be today. I like to think I would have found other ways to get new business, but I hate being a salesperson, so I may not still be in business today.

Bottom line: By providing your assistant with an ongoing window into your mind, you're giving them a leg up in understanding who you are and what you need, which ultimately helps them do a better job for you.

Note that when it comes to these kinds of referrals, most people don't ask for any sort of fee. When you make an introduction to a great prospective client, you're likely to be reciprocated with a direct referral to your business or another useful recommendation to another service provider in the future. This is often more valuable than a referral fee. Everybody wins!

4. Use Technology to Make Work Smarter

Technology can be a bit daunting, especially now that the internet officially has ALL THE THINGS. It's almost impossible to decide which tool to use for what and when to use it with so many options out there. The last thing I want is for you to feel constricted by a lack of technological skills, industry knowledge, or experience.

You certainly don't *need* lots of tools to succeed with a VA. More often than not, your VA will come equipped with a corral of tools of their own and they likely won't need to you provide any of them. If you're shy about setting up your own accounts for these tools, you're more than welcome to use the technology that your assistant already has.

The only thing that you need to be careful of is ownership and privacy. I wouldn't want you to do an hour-long training session on how you handle your billing and invoicing only to have your assistant leave abruptly, taking the recording of that training with them.

Losing a training video, of course, is an innocent example. The files, processes, and private information the VA could take with them, either accidentally or deliberately, could be catastrophic.

To keep things simple, it's best if you, as the client, can take the recommendations of your VA and set up your own accounts on the apps and tools you need. This way, you can control the content and can maintain ownership of everything yourself.

I'm always wary of recommending tools because everyone works differently, so the way I use a tool might not work for you. In the appendix, I share a comprehensive list of tools that my team and I use to get work done and share the pros, cons, and costs of each so you have an arsenal of solutions at your fingertips and can implement them accordingly. In the meantime, I wanted to share a few favorites to get you started:

Communications

Sococo: A virtual office tool that allows you to see who's "online" and working, but not in a creepy way. This tool allows for text, voice, and video chat, plus screen share. http://sococo.com

Zoom: A common web conferencing service. This tool allows you to schedule conference calls using a phone dial-in and VoIP. Screen sharing, video, and voice options available. http://zoom.com

Loom: Zoom? Loom? Vroom?? Someone had that "oom" on the mind when they created my favorite tools. Loom allows you to quickly create videos to explain or train on something and then share a link to your team. http://useloom.com

Project Management

Trello: An online board tool that allows you to create virtual post-it notes for each project and easily move them through to completion. http://trello.com

Asana: A basic, affordable project management tool that integrates with Gmail for ease of use. This is Don't Panic Management's project management tool of choice as of the day I'm writing this, though we've tried many, many others over the years. http://asana.com

Calendar & Scheduling

Google Calendar: Google, the best friend you've always wanted. This is a common service of choice for many businesses that operate using Google Apps and we lurv it. http://calendar.google.com

Calendly: Integrate your own calendar and set your desired meeting availability with this tool in order to get a shareable link that allows people to schedule meetings with you. Simple and free. http://calendly.com

Email Marketing

Mailchimp: This is the small biz dream tool for email marketing. It's free up until a certain number of subscribers and makes creating templates and sending email newsletters a breeze. http://mailchimp.com

ConvertKit: A newer tool, ConvertKit makes it easier to segment, send to unopens, and create visual automations than Mailchimp. It's a better solution if you have a lot of personalizations, want to create landing pages, or even sell things through email. http://convertkit.com

Business Tools

Gusto: Payroll made easy. Gusto allows you to pay employees and contractors with friendly branding and customer service. They also file certain state and federal reports for you and have incorporated benefits like health insurance in certain states. http://gusto.com

Harvest: Time tracking like a boss! Harvest allows easy time tracking from desktop or mobile. It also integrates with lots of complementary tools, including Asana, so you can track time against a specific project. http://getharvest.com

Quickbooks Online: If you've outgrown Freshbooks, this is the tool for you. Quickbooks Online integrates with your bank/credit card system for easy expense tracking and categorizing, plus easy invoicing and payment. http://quickbooks.intuit.com/online/

Traveling Mailbox: For when you hate checking the mail as much as I do (and you don't want to set your home address as your business address when you're a virtual company), Traveling Mailbox will open and scan your mail for you, delivering it to your inbox as a PDF. You can also have important documents or checks forwarded for a small fee. http://travelingmailbox.com

There are more details about all of these tools in the Appendix, and I hope you take the time to test and implement some of these tools to make your business and your relationship with your VA run even smoother.

The key with any tool is to actually *use* it. That's why many tools offer a free 15-day or 30-day trial. From my perspective, the best trial time would be 21 days. That's the amount of time it takes to form a habit. And that's what using these tools becomes: a habit! They won't work for you any other way.

While using these tools and strategies, you may feel like your VA runs your business at times. This is awesome!

Never forget that you are in charge. You are the boss. Thus, you set the tone of how the relationship will (or will not) thrive.

Your attitude, your commitment to communication, and your enthusiasm for developing a relationship that lasts can be seen and felt by everyone on your team. Don't take this unique opportunity for granted. Instead, use this opportunity to cultivate a partnership with a VA that genuinely cares about you and your business. You won't be sorry.

In the next section, we'll take the FU out of FUN and make sure that your crazy successful work life includes some joy as well.

chapter fourteen

YOU RAISE ME UP

No one can deny Josh Groban's ability to make even the darkest situations brighter when you hear his voice: "You raise me up so I can stand on mountains! You raise me up to walk on stormy seas!"

Put that song on your Spotify right now and tell me you don't feel immediately inspired. Whether it's a funeral or a wedding, this song somehow is appropriate for almost any situation. It's pretty impressive, if you ask me.

I hope you've started to understand my philosophy on what makes a virtual assistant relationship work. If I had to put it in simple terms, it's a combo pack of hard work, strong communication, and not being a dick. When you get it right, it can feel like you're high fiving a million angels, Tina Fey style.

So what's the icing on the cake? How can you REALLY solidify the relationship and keep you and your assistant swimming happily along with the tide forever?

Celebrations. Appreciations. The opposite of altercations, whatever that is. Hugs, maybe?

Yes. I'm talking champagne and glitter.

Or if you don't like champagne, tequila and balloons. Or if you don't like alcohol, grapefruit La Croix and cupcakes.

You catch my drift.

Cupcakes, champagne, balloons, glitter . . . these things have no real purpose in life other than to make us feel good. And when we feel good, we are nicer to people. And when we are nicer to other people, we are better managers. And when we're better managers, we run better businesses. And when we run better businesses, we make more money.

So that we can buy more cupcakes, champagne, balloons, and glitter.

It's a glorious happiness loop, wouldn't you say?

I get that you can't possibly celebrate all day every day because then you'd just be a drunk. Drunk on sugar. Drunk on glitter. Drunk on shots of tequila. Hard work generally happens when we're sober and focused. So besides champagne, what are some other ways we can celebrate and keep the happiness loop moving around and around?

Create a Positive Community

What were once seen as solely an IRL phenomenon, communities exist all over the internet now. Our ancestors wouldn't believe it. They were limited to the people in their village and nothing more. Now, you can find an online community for anything you're interested in, from knitting to organic dog treats.

There's a reason these communities are so powerful: They make us feel less alone. And somehow, in this wild world of connectivity, we feel more alone than ever.

Millennials are particularly plagued by this problem because they've grown up with the internet. According to a 2011 study, 86 percent of millennials reported feeling lonely and depressed[1]. A 2014 study uncovered

1. Hill, Amelia. "The quarterlife crisis: young, insecure and depressed." *The Guardian*, 5 May 2011, www.theguardian.com/society/2011/may/05/quarterlife-crisis-young-insecure-depressed.

that 18- to 24-year-olds were four times as likely to feel lonely all the time than older generations[1].

This is likely to continue in the years to come, which makes creating positive communities today more important than ever.

Communities can take many forms. When a company is completely virtual and has multiple staff members and/or contractors, it makes sense to create an online community just for the team to take part in. These generally run best on a Slack channel or private Facebook group. If you have more than ten or so team members, you may want to consider putting someone in charge of managing the community. That could be your director of HR, your social media coordinator, or whoever generally acts the most like your team's head cheerleader.

In Don't Panic's case, our Chief People Officer is our community manager. She always responds to everyone's posts and questions and is in charge of posting prompts in the group when there's a lull in activity. Motivation Monday is a popular one, as is the weekly "share your current feelings using only a GIF" thread.

When we're working deep in a challenging project or filtering through an annoying request, simply posting that we're frustrated to the group relieves some of the

---

1. Sanghani, Radhika. "Generation Lonely: Britain's young people have never been less connected." *The Telegraph*, 28 Dec. 2014, www.telegraph.co.uk/women/womens-life/11312075/Generation-Lonely-Britains-young-people-have-never-been-less-connected.html.

stress. Oftentimes the act of venting to a community of team members that get what we're going through is enough to change the story we're telling ourselves. It helps us face tough issues and makes us feel supported and empowered enough to get through it together.

You may be wondering about the celebration element in this example. Well, that was the main reason for the group's inception! In the beginning, we only posted on Fridays. On Fridays, we would share our "rock star moments" from the week. These were the times when we felt like total badasses, whether it be knocking a huge project off the list, getting a client to make a decision about a flight plan, finally, or even getting a newborn to sleep through the night.

This list of awesome accomplishments included the occasional breakthrough moment, but for the most part was comprised of small, seemingly menial things, but things that mattered to the success of our work. While this list of things wasn't something that we would share publicly with the entire world (after all, most of our friends and family wouldn't understand what we were even talking about), it was a mighty list of achievements that we could pat each other on the back for and make each and every team member feel valued.

A secondary benefit to the community is that it helps us get to know each other. As we are well aware, knowing someone more personally builds trust. Trust creates tighter relationships. Tighter personal relationships cause better working relationships. And better working relationships? Well, you know the rest.

I know that posting rock star moments in a private Facebook group each week doesn't necessarily make a better team. It's not a direct A to B scenario here and a lot of people don't want to waste time doing things that don't provide an immediate result. I'm super impatient so I get it, I really do. But whether you have one VA, a bookkeeper, and yourself, or five VAs, three executives, and 20 employees, online communities are a great way to promote celebrations if you are intentional about cultivating that sort of culture.

It doesn't have to be a private Facebook group. It could be a Slack thread or text message chain. It could just be a quick email to your VA telling them they did a great job. Or a carrier pigeon dropping off a note of thanks.

I wish I had tracked retention among team members before and after we adopted Sococo and the Facebook group because I firmly believe we would see an increase in retention *and* happiness, if we could measure it, after creating and developing our little community.

Never Forget a Birthday

When you care about someone, you remember things about them. Your mom's favorite flower, for example. Or your dad's favorite brand of coffee. Or your wife's biggest pet peeve. (That's an important one!)

You remember these things because people feel loved when they feel like you're listening to them and taking their needs and wants into account.

Also, gifts. Everyone loves a good gift. Something they actually want, of course (not junk).

I like to set aside a "happiness" budget with my team. Each month, we have some money (think $50 to $150) to brighten someone's day. Whether they're going through a hard family situation like a death or illness, or they've gone above and beyond on a new client project or knocked it out of the park on a blog post, small gifts go a long way in making someone feel appreciated, loved, and included.

Or maybe it's their birthday! Birthdays deserve to be celebrated.

A lot of people don't think about it this way, but oftentimes your VA knows you more intimately than many, many other people in your life. They see your preferences and your schedules, your bank accounts and your profit and loss statements. They know the inner workings of your brain.

You may not always recognize how important this is, but imagine for a moment what would happen if that information was shared or lost or compromised? Be grateful for what your assistant does for you each and every day. If you can't remember to be grateful each and every day (and say something about it), well then at least take one day per year, like a birthday or a big holiday (perhaps Administrative Professionals' Day), to do so. Your efforts will not go unnoticed and your assistant will appreciate feeling like their ongoing work for you actually means something.

By the way, this is good-human-training here, not just good-VA-manager training. Feel free to take these strategies into your home as well!

Get Outside

I won't lie: The main reason I go to spin class and get out for a run four to five times per week is so I can eat cheese and drink wine and not weigh 300 pounds.

The other reasons are probably related to why most people exercise. Exercise promotes heart health and boosts endorphins. Endorphins make you happy. And happy people just don't shoot their husbands! *Legally Blonde* fans, anyone? No? Okay, just me . . .

When heart disease is the number one killer of both men and women, I'd say that getting that blood flowing is pretty important for all of us. Remember, you can't run your business if you're dead. Nope, nope, nope.

Outdoor exercise especially encourages mental wellness as well, and some people even use their exercise time to get into a meditative state. I'll admit this has yet to work for me, but I'm still trying.

The reason exercise is so powerful for a lot of business owners and entrepreneurs is that it forces a brain break. It makes you get up from your desk and move your body. And even 20 to 30 minutes every day can make a huge difference in your mental and physical well-being, which promotes feelings of gratitude and appreciation.

Plus, you know how you always get those great big ideas when you're in the shower and you have no idea where they came from and nowhere to write them down? (If you have an Alexa or Google Home hooked up near your bathroom you can always call out to have them jot down the idea in a note!) That's because when our brains are idle, they have space to wander. This is when all the biggest ideas are formed (whether they're crazy or not, that's another story).

Going on a walk, run, or hike can give you that physical space away from your desk and away from your work to let your mind wander. You're allowing yourself to think about all the wonderful things that happen each day. I always recommend not bringing your phone with you when you do this so you can truly let go. Don't be afraid to mark your calendar for when you're going to exercise so everyone, including your assistant, knows you won't be available during this time.

Don't feel guilty about it. Get a FitBit, Apple Watch, or other fitness tracker to keep on your wrist if you're counting steps.

For most people, spending 20, 30, or even 60 minutes away and unavailable is not going to result in a life or death situation. (Unless you're an on-call doctor, then please, take your phone or whatever beeper situation hospitals use these days to stay in touch!) The benefits of just that short window of time are often immeasurable. Use this precious time to appreciate the fact that you have your health and that you have a support system that can be there for your business even when you're not.

Try it and tell me you don't feel more clarity in your work and in your life. You might even shed a few pounds along the way. Bonus!

Balance Isn't a Real Thing (But Take Breaks Anyway)

People are always talking about work/life balance these days. That term was never a thing until we started working more than we were living. This is typically an American problem—the Europeans are great at taking long lunches and afternoon siestas. It is a problem because we are more stressed and sick than ever. According to a 2017 study, 8.3 million American adults, which is about 3.4 percent of the U.S. population, suffer from "serious psychological distress."[1] Mental illness and suicide rates are on the rise. My 2014 Cycle of Sick is a small example of what's going on in our society.

In addition to setting my priorities (family, health, team), the only other way I've been able to combat this challenge is to schedule everything, including breaks. For me, I tend to work for a few hours first thing in the morning before my first break. That break is when I make breakfast, take the dog for an hour walk, and listen to a podcast or two.

When I'm back at my desk, most people are starting to rise and respond to my emails. This is when I start any

---

1. "Study Paints Somber Picture of U.S. Mental Health Status & Access to Care." *NYU Langone Health*, 17 Apr. 2017, nyulangone.org/press-releases/study-paints-somber-picture-of-us-mental-health-status-access-to-care.

meetings or phone calls. Meetings, emails, writing, and other projects usually take a few more hours, and then I go take my run or get to the gym if I didn't already do an early morning spin class before my first work block.

After I'm back from that, I may check in one more time and tie up any loose ends before retiring for the evening, making dinner, and spending time with my cohabitants.

In this way, I'm never working for more than four or so hours in a row, which is very different from where I started—working from morning to night without more than a few pee breaks and maybe a microwaved meal.

The breaks are great for my mental health, but they also provide me time to reflect. I think about my to-do list, sure, and I also think about my people. "Man, Becca has really put in a lot of hours these last few days. I'm going to offer her a day off this week." Or, "Wow, Jenn did a lot of extra work on that project to make sure it was perfect. I'm going to suggest she takes a long weekend next week." And so on. Time off—whether it's a day, an hour, or an afternoon—is a gift.

The frenetic energy I used to feel going from one meeting to another hasn't completely left me. There are some days (usually Mondays and Tuesdays) when I load up on work and meetings and it gets a little crazy. But for me, frontloading the week allows me to take it a little easier come Wednesday. My goal is always to take Fridays off, or at least make them half-days. Taking the day off completely hardly ever works, but I do have fewer deadlines and important tasks to worry about come Friday because I've worked my butt off Monday, Tuesday, and Wednesday.

Everyone is different, so if you're going to offer time off as a reward, let the time be on your assistant's own terms, not yours.

I don't have an endless fountain of energy, and neither do you. We can work hard, but we need breaks. We need slower times. This is why the weekend was invented right? Sundays? Day of rest and all that?

Look, I'm not saying you have to subscribe to society's view of "normal" when it comes to work hours. Hell, I work at least a little bit every day, whether it's Tuesday or Saturday. For me, checking in and staying ahead (or at least attempting to) is what minimizes my anxiety, so that's what I need. And I encourage the following idea for everyone:

Listen to your body to quiet your mind.

If you're exhausted because you were up late worrying about something, well, fix that thing and then take a nap. You can't be effective if you're dragging. Close your eyes for 20 minutes and move on. Don't tell me that whatever other thing you were trying to do can't wait. Trust me, nine times out of ten, it can!

There are tons of ways to celebrate the amazing accomplishments that you and your assistant achieve, no matter how big or how small they are. The important thing is to recognize what they are and when they happen. I remember having my head buried in a mountain of projects, feeling like no one knew how hard I was working or whether or not I was even getting anything done. At the end of that project, I got a "thanks" or a "good work," but nothing more. That was enough for me at the time, but the "wow" moments came when I received an unexpected card, a small bouquet of flowers, or a $5 Starbucks gift card for something I was sure that my client had overlooked.

Those are the times when I say to myself, "I love what I do."

These days, I give myself the day off for my birthday as a gift for my own accomplishments, which I think is just as important as celebrating other people's birthdays. I send surprise cards and gifts just because I'm grateful. I try to remember to say something nice about someone on my team via Facebook, email, or text, at least once a week. And while these small gestures are no skin off my back, they make all the difference to the person on the receiving end. Ultimately, are the glue to the bond that keeps you and your assistant together forever.

conclusion

KEEP CALM AND CARRY ON

Today, I took a hard look at my calendar. It's full of walks with my pup, spinning workouts with good friends, happy hours on the porch, meetings with new clients, concerts, lunch-and-learns led by different team members, brainstorming sessions, lots of writing and editing time, rehearsals with the band I play in, and tons of weddings and events with friends. I'm also in the midst of planning my own wedding, so various appointments and to-dos take up a couple hours each week.

Almost everything I do these days is something I love to do or is within my unique value proposition as CEO.

We've implemented revenue and profit goals for the next three years and we've determined which initiatives we need to complete in order to reach those goals. Every quarter, each member of the full-time team takes a week to "sprint" toward their initiatives. With our heads down and our eyes on the prize, we've accomplished more now than ever before.

I had never been able to accomplish so many big projects before because I didn't have the time or energy to think about goals, assign initiatives, or get any help ensuring that they get done. The only way I'm able to reach my big, hairy, audacious goals today is because I've taken my own advice and released my tightly-gripped claws from every single little thing that my business needs to run.

I can only imagine what today would look like if I never got the help that I really didn't want, but truly needed, back in 2014.

First, I wouldn't have been able to achieve nearly as much growth for the business . . . if any. Back then, there was barely enough time to do the client work I already had, let alone try to find new clients. In addition to hiring my very first full-time employee, who is now our Chief People Officer, I have been able to hone in on the big-picture philosophy for what I want the company to be when it grows up. Therefore, the team and I have been able to determine the kinds of people that will be the best fits for us, both on the client-facing side and on the virtual assistant side.

This has helped us grow intentionally, with very minimal turnover on the VA side and fewer headaches on the client side. Almost 100 percent of our roster is happy, well-cared for, and feels like they're getting what they need from working with us. At least as far as I know. And we do a lot of surveys, so if someone isn't telling me something that's their problem!

Everyone is happier because we are making better matches. We aren't working with folks who don't meet our criteria and we aren't hiring assistants who don't share our values. This isn't because we're trying to leave people out or because we don't want to help them. This is because we know who we are and who we are best suited to help. The truth is that our services aren't for everyone, and it's taken a long time for the pleaser in me to admit that's part of running a business. You can't be all things to all people.

Instead of forcing every ingredient into a recipe that only we know how to bake, we make the recipe publicly accessible for everyone to see. If your ingredients list doesn't fit ours, that's okay! There's another restaurant with another recipe that will be perfect for you. In fact, we're happy to recommend them to you. But we wouldn't have been able to do that without refining our own recipe first.

Second, I wouldn't have hired my Chief Client Officer. She did such a great job putting forth her best qualities during a casual interview that I took a chance and made her my intern. She was patient and helpful, forcing me out of my comfort zone and allowing her to take scheduling off my plate to start. She controlled the madness with her calendaring, reminder, and, dare I say, nagging skills, which helped everyone stay on track. Then, she got some of the backlogged content marketing activities done, including posting old blog posts to my LinkedIn profile and scheduling some social media posts. Then, she solved every problem I had been using weird hacks to get around with some ninja Googling skills.

And the rest is history!

She proved herself so competent, driven, and a culturally great fit for my style that I couldn't help but hire her to help me full-time. We've never looked back. She's helped countless clients with last-minute emergencies, has kept all the money and contracts in order (which, frankly, is one of the hardest things we do), and has been a steady, immovable force by always sticking to her guns and not letting the company get undercut by nasty clients who want work done for free.

Finally, and perhaps most importantly, I wouldn't be writing this book right now. I wouldn't have the experience and perspective to be able to share how to thrive in a world that is only going to move more in the direction of virtual support and remote work.

From reluctantly learning how to let go and stop being such a micromanager to training both clients and VAs to play nicely together, it's been a whirlwind roller coaster ride that I never could have imagined. I've met raconteurs and entrepreneurs, actors and chefs, baby-growers and trapeze artists. I've looked fear in the eye and said, "SCREW YOU, FEAR!" and gone along to do the things I'm terrified of doing in spite of myself. (Writing this book being one of them!)

I've grown and changed and pissed people off and saved their lives all at the same time. I've graduated from the days when my mom was sending me job clippings to the day when she watched me speak on an international stage about how VAs are going to save the world. And I'm proud to say that in spite of my fierce independence, I haven't done it alone.

Neither should you.

If nothing else, I hope you feel a little calmer knowing the path to virtual assistant success. But if you're still uneasy, just try to remember these three things:

1. You Deserve to Live Pain-Free

Sometimes, the pain of staying where you are is worse than the pain of making a change.

For a while, I found ways to ease the pain of 80-hour work weeks. You know, things like Friday happy hour and binge-watching *Game of Thrones* and keeping my calendar insanely full so I never had a chance to stop and experience any kind of emotion at all.

I was a walking zombie, not enjoying life but not hating it either. In fact, I was pretty numb. I thought that the way to success was burying my needs into the ground, ignoring physical warning signs, and being as busy as possible.

That's what I saw my mentors and heroes doing, at least on the surface. Social media has a way of hiding what's really going on, you know what I mean?

But just because going 1,000 miles per minute forever works for some people doesn't mean it has to work for you. You deserve to design a life you love. You deserve to make your passion possible. You deserve to have someone help you do it. (Remember, Superhero Syndrome is NOT a good look!)

So, yes, you're right, taking unnecessary things off your plate, automating every part of your workflow that you possibly can, and even hiring someone for all the rest is going to be painful. I know it is. It's going to feel unnatural and it's going to disrupt your rhythm and you're going to want to give up.

But don't. Remember that all of the time and money and energy you put into these processes is temporary. It might take months or even years for you to reap the full benefits of your efforts, but you WILL reap them. Mark my words. Because you'll do the thing that I did at the beginning of this section. You'll look at your calendar and you'll breathe a sigh of relief knowing that at least 90 percent of the things on there are things you personally love and want to be doing for the betterment of your business and your life.

2. You're Not Performing Brain Surgery

When a client sends me an emergency text that their website crashed or they are 100 percent convinced the airplane they're sitting on is going to spontaneously combust, I take a deep breath, another sip of wine, and I think, "What can I do to make this better?"

Being solutions-oriented as opposed to problems-oriented is a great way to get through any dark day. Remembering that other people perform actual brain surgery and save people's lives is a great way to put whatever you're struggling with into perspective.

I remember when I was doing that volunteer AmeriCorps program called City Year, one of our leaders told us to "fake it 'til you make it." I hated this saying for the longest time. I thought it was total bullshit. Why would I fake my attitude? I was pissed off all the time about waking up early and taking shitty L.A. public transportation and dealing with mean children who refuse to do their homework. I was sick and tired of doing jumping jacks in the middle of downtown and I was frustrated that I couldn't afford to pay for a bottle of wine.

But there was something to that little saying, I begrudgingly learned. When she told me to smile, even if I didn't want to, I started to feel better. When she told me to just pretend like I was having fun, eventually I did.

Ultimately, it's not a strategy that works forever. If you're finding that you have to fake some level of positivity day in and day out for weeks or months, well, that takes a lot of energy and probably tells you that you're not doing what you should be doing. Instead, if you can take an extra second to check your attitude, remind yourself that you are not, in fact, performing brain surgery and that no one is going to live or die, your mental wellness will be in a much better place. As a bonus, keeping that attitude day in and day out is what keeps morale and motivation high among your team, and that goes a long way in maintaining long-lasting relationships.

3. Sometimes It's a Good Idea to Jump Off a Cliff

Remember when I told you about my first client, Jay Baer?

Well, technically, this was all his idea. It seemed like an offhand comment at first. He said something like, "Why don't you make this a real agency so you can offer services to more people?"

I remember being taken aback. What? Me?? Starting a company?? Uh uh. No way, Jose.

Sure, I studied entrepreneurship and business and marketing in college, but I had never actually started a business before. How would I know what to do? What would I do if something went wrong? If I lost all my money? My reputation?

Or worse . . . what would I do if everything went right?

For me, the scariest thing was not failure. It was success. I didn't know how to handle praise, let alone a burgeoning businesses with tens of clients and assistants to take care of on a daily basis. Keeping people happy? Providing their livelihood? Changing the world?? Terrifying!

And yet, here we are. I know that my tiny company isn't actually changing the world, but we are changing lives. I know that because of the things that clients and VAs alike have said to me. I know that because of the recommendations and referrals we receive every single day. And I know that because the numbers don't lie.

When we make the right match between client and VA, business grows. Maybe not at first. Maybe the investment of hiring the VA causes the bottom line number to shrink for a month or two. But then? It's hours back in your day that you can use to earn more revenue. The revenue you earn is at a higher hourly rate than what you pay for your assistant. Soon, the hours you're able to bill out or the number of widgets you're able to create with your newfound time outweigh the investment you're putting toward your VA and your bottom line number rises.

By reading this book, you've positioned yourself in that very place—to make the smart investment in your business, your time, your life, and, ultimately, the lives of those around you.

Take that first step into what feels like the unknown. Be patient. Fall hard. Fall fast. Feel confident knowing that you've done your homework, you've done the necessary preparation, and there will be a soft net at the bottom to catch you and give you a nice, big hug.

So, you know, don't panic.

:)

finale

YOU ARE SUPPORTING AN ECONOMY OF WORLD-CHANGERS

I would simply LOVE to tell you about all the ways virtual assistants make an impact on the world. I'm not just talking about for their clients, but for other human beings, the environment, and society as a whole.

My words can't do justice to the words that come from their hearts. So I wanted to leave you with a few stories from real VAs doing real work, not only for Don't Panic Management, but also for the greater good.

Changing the World Through Art
By Elise LeBreton, Content, Graphics, and Project Management VA

I moved to New York City the fall after I finished graduate school. I had a master's degree in acting, an apartment, a box full of resumés, and a whole lot of hustling to do to find my next acting opportunity. I needed a "thrival" job that would support me while I searched. My dream job, as I envisioned it, would allow me to flex my non-fine arts skills and would be there for me as other gigs came and went.

I found that dream job working as a virtual assistant with Don't Panic Management.

Like many folks in the performing arts, I'm a self-employed creator who wears a few different hats (metaphorical hats, that is, though I sometimes wear literal hats too). I perform with theatres in New York City and on the west coast, I write plays and musicals, I read and evaluate scripts for Off-Broadway theatres—and that's just an average Wednesday. It's thrilling and more fulfilling than words can express.

This kind of creative career also means that providing for myself financially has taken some, well, creativity.

The Cold, Hard Truth of Making a Living in the Arts

An enormous percentage of working actors, visual artists, musicians, poets, dancers, and others make their living from some combination of paid artistic work and supplementary jobs. Those jobs often include things like adjunct teaching, personal assisting, babysitting, tutoring, bartending, and (the old classic) waiting tables.

A successful artist's income often doesn't follow a linear upward trajectory, either. There's a common narrative that after an artist's "big break," they can subsist solely on their paid artistic work and never need to wait another table.

This doesn't reflect most artists' realities, however— even Lin-Manuel Miranda, one of the most decorated artists of the decade, was still writing restaurant reviews for a local newspaper after his first musical (the one before *Hamilton*) became a hit on Broadway.

The rise of the gig economy, for all its drawbacks, has been a boon for folks like me—never have there been so many diverse opportunities for freelance work and part-time skilled labor. Instead of job-hopping my way through the food service industry, I have the option to bring my arsenal of creative skills to a small business I care about, like Don't Panic.

The benefits of this work aren't a one-way street, either: My time with Don't Panic has also taught me new skills I wouldn't have the chance to develop otherwise.

The VA Life Has Made Me More Self-Motivated

When I joined Don't Panic, I underestimated the serious learning curve that accompanies working remotely for the first time. A great remote VA is exceptionally self-motivated, a master of time management, a solid communicator, and comfortable working alone. It's a unique suite of skills that takes real effort to master.

It's also the same suite of skills every self-employed creative needs to stay productive. So much of my artistic hustle happens without an authority figure standing over my shoulder. It's up to me to find that next audition, finish writing that script, fill out that residency application, or brainstorm my next project. My work as a VA has made me a better, more driven artist.

My VA Clients Teach Me About Other Industries

Thanks to my diverse corral of clients, I get glimpses into a huge variety of industries, from tech and finance to marketing, publishing, and public relations. I know more about maintaining a food truck than I ever thought I would.

My work in these areas has shown me the magical things that happen when industries cross-pollinate, and how a team of diverse perspectives leads to better problem-solving and heightened creativity. It always dismays me how frequently the business and art worlds misunderstand and misrepresent each other; these days, I often find myself being the person in the room who bridges that gap in understanding.

(It's also wildly useful at parties! People are often surprised when I want to talk about their work as a UI developer or social video producer, but I love being able to ask meaningful questions about what other folks do all day.)

My Creative Career Doesn't Feel Extra-Curricular

As a professional, I'm not interested in relegating my creative career to weekends or late nights. Working remotely as a contractor means I have tremendous flexibility in when and where I work, whether that day's· work includes designing an ebook for a client or going to a costume fitting.

When my acting career takes me out of town, my "thrival" job can travel with me.

When I signed on to develop a new musical with my colleagues, I didn't have to put my VA work on hold.

I don't have to worry where my next paycheck will come from when I'm between artistic projects—my clients will be there. This work offers me a bit of rare, much-needed security as I navigate an otherwise unpredictable career path.

When I left school and began my career as a self-employed artist, I knew I was signing on to a life of constant hustle, long hours, and uncertainty. My work as a VA allows me to provide for myself despite that uncertainty—a rare opportunity that makes my wild, ever-changing career journey just a little easier.

Changing the World Through Life
An Interview with Kimberly Voorhis, Admin and Project Management VA

If you had checked in with Kimberly Voorhis four years ago, you might have met a spirited, friendly newlywed commuting hours a day to her office job. She was out the door at 5:30 a.m. to beat SoCal rush hour traffic, she worked seven to five, and didn't make it home until 6:30 or 7:00 each night. Fourteen hour days were the norm, no matter how much work was (or wasn't) on her plate. "No matter what, I would have to sit at my desk until 5 o'clock. Even if I was done at 2 o'clock."

Two years ago? She was deep in the weeds of the California foster care system, working as a freelance virtual assistant from courthouse waiting rooms, social worker appointments, and parental visits inside any agreed-upon place with wifi.

Today, she and her husband Mark are the forever parents to three beautiful kids ages 7, 6, and almost 3 (and, as of this article's publishing, have opened their home and hearts at one time or another to 6 other babies in the foster system). So much has changed, but she's still pretty spirited and friendly.

Kimberly is more than just a VA. She's also a mom, a foster caretaker, and a temporary source of love and respite for some of California's youngest weary souls.

"I Was Told It Would Be Hard."

When Kimberly and Mark first felt called to become foster parents, she was warned about working a traditional 9-to-5 schedule. "When we first started, we had been told it was possible—it would be hard but it would be possible—to foster and work." But, as any of our readers on the west coast know, trying to pay a mortgage on a single income in Southern California is almost impossible. Both Kimberly and Mark tried to make it work.

Their first placement was a newborn baby boy. Kimberly used her paid maternity leave to care for him.

And then she hit a roadblock when they received their second placement: a 3-month old little boy.

"I didn't have any leave left. Even if I were to have a biological child, I didn't have any time left, or it was unpaid. When we got [my son], I had to go back to work the next day and place him in an in-home daycare."

She was working long hours with a difficult commute, and she didn't have any resources at her job she could utilize to care for her new baby. She had used up every scrap of leave already.

Several months later, when she got the call that her little boy had two older sisters who also needed a home, Kimberly had two thoughts. First: in a short window, she and Mark moved from having no children to having three. Second: her job wasn't going to be able to support the huge life-changing event she was in the throes of.

So, she decorated the spare bedroom with two twin beds—and she quit her job.

"The Tradeoff Is Forever."

Around the same time, a friend introduced her to Don't Panic. Kimberly didn't know jobs like this even existed. She thought contractor work was for people with design degrees or highly-specialized skills.

The next few years are a blur of client meetings and social worker meetings, calendar management for her job and calendar management for her kids. She won't say that working from home as a virtual assistant made fostering easy. Sometimes, on her busiest days, she was up around 4 a.m., just so she could squeeze in a cup of coffee by herself before she kicked off her crazy schedule.

But the flexibility and the ability to be with her kids, plus being able to contribute to her household, has been invaluable. As she puts it, "I can do anything that's temporary, knowing there's a light at the end of the tunnel. The tradeoff is 'forever.' Whether your foster experience lasts one year or ten years and you see hundreds of kids, it's worth it."

December 19, 2016

On December 19, 2016, after over two years of fostering, Kimberly and Mark were finally able to adopt their kids. While they still occasionally open their home and their hearts to little ones in need, life is generally a lot calmer. Like most moms who work at home, she gets most of her work done while her kids are at school. In the afternoons, she closes her laptop and takes them to the beach, or to Starbucks for a quick treat, or they make dinner together as a family. When we spoke on the phone for this interview, she was checking in with me from a short vacation before another school year kicks off.

The relief in her voice is palpable when she talks about this new chapter in their lives. "I feel like I'm living in a different world."

"There Is a Way to Do It All."

Kimberly's biggest piece of advice for people looking to move from a more traditional work life to something virtual is to find your tribe. Working with an agency was incredibly helpful when she was in the trenches of her foster journey. Unexpected calls from social workers or parental visitations that ran late meant having a support system and flexibility in her work was essential. She found that at Don't Panic. "I had people to lean on if there was an emergency."

She encourages anyone feeling called to undergo a huge change like becoming a foster parent to do their research and explore how they might want their career to adapt as well. Most people don't realize that it's possible to finish your work day by noon and spend the afternoon building sand castles with your kids. But those jobs exist out there if you know where to find them!

"There is a way to do it all, and do it all well."

Changing the World Through Parenting
By Briana Barrios, Admin VA

My story starts with a burrito. That's right, a burrito. My all-time favorite burrito from a place down the street, in fact. You know, one of those unassuming little hole-in-the-wall gems that turn out legit amazing Mexican food (and my personal go-to on nights I didn't feel like cooking . . . and often the reason I didn't want to cook in the first place).

On this particular night, this jewel of bean and cheese, well, let's just say, didn't sit well. And it marked the beginning of the biggest change in my life.

For when this burrito walked through my door all of a sudden I could smell every scent in the room. The dogs smelled horrible, plus I could swear we were hiding salami under the couch or something. I was pretty convinced I had either developed some sort of superhero quality that I wanted gone, or the high school down the street held football practice in our living room that afternoon.

There it was. My smelly burrito was hint number one . . . I was pregnant!

In hindsight I guess maybe a normal person would have gotten the hint, and all the ones to follow, but I was pretty clueless. After all, I hadn't gone to Europe yet, I just got married, and hello! Type A personality! Nothing was slipping by me without first being on my calendar! You all know how the story goes.

Needless to say, prenatal vitamins, cankles, and 40 weeks later, she was here.

Here's the thing though: During this time, I basically had no idea how on earth we were going to make this situation work financially. Lord knows I really wanted to be a stay-at-home momma, but the reality was that I need to work.

That's when Don't Panic Management (DPM) came in. A friend told me about the company, and long story short, I'm sure my vocabulary is not even sophisticated enough to describe the saving grace that working as a virtual assistant has been. Let me tell you why.

1. Flexibility

Oh, you have 800 prenatal appointments? You want to go on a hike? You forgot something at the store for a dinner you were just told you had to host...tonight? No problem!

Seriously, the biggest benefit of the VA life is flexibility. I know the hours I have to put in ahead of time, I do them, and no one on the client end even knows it all happens during naptime—while I sip my tea, with the laundry going, and my favorite podcast on. (Who am I kidding? The baby is screaming in the background because she doesn't want to sleep. But at least I have that flexibility to go give her a bit of comfort, right?)

Stay-at-home moms have it hard. Working moms have it hard. The flexibility of freelancing makes it all a little bit easier: you really can't beat having the ability to care for your family both financially and physically.

Also, real talk. I have zero commute, can wear stretchy pants on the daily, and I basically can't remember the last time I wore makeup. Win, win, win.

2. Ongoing Education

Here's sort of an unexpected side effect of being a virtual assistant. If you're willing, you can learn far more than you would be able to at other jobs. I realize that sounds silly. But track with me.

Over the course of working with DPM I've had, let's say, six clients. Although their workflows all fall roughly within my skill set, they are all 100 percent different people at different companies with totally different ways of doing things. Each comes with unique preferences, organizational tools, hacks, apps, and tasks. I literally went from being great at "scheduling meetings and booking flights" to learning marketing strategies, SEO, pitch writing, and more.

I've now become an "expert" (at least in my own mind) on topics I was asked to research. I've worked with a dozen personalities who each need their own specific needs heard and met. I've become a student of their businesses, soaking in all I can to not only be a better employee for them, but also be more knowledgeable for my own career. I literally got training on everything I could need to start a business by helping other people with theirs.

Between interacting with all the various clients, and being led by an awesome internal team, the opportunities for growth, learning, and taking on new challenges is around every corner. This is great for stay-at-home parents because hustling to go back to school with little ones is seriously tough. I'm continuing my education with on-the-job training while my little girl sits on my lap. It's thrilling!

3. Balance

I know work is just a part of life. It's the norm to be in a 9-to-5 where you go in early and come home late. And the reality is most fields are like that. But what if it didn't have to be? What if more of us weren't just working to survive, we were working to thrive?

Being a VA-slash-SAHM (Stay At Home Mom) has brought a new sense of balance to my life. My whole life doesn't revolve around work. I got the balance back. I work, I take care of my family, I exercise. I can make meals, do laundry, dance around to an unidentifiable genre of music, meet people for coffee, and hit up the farmers market before all the good stuff is gone. I can pull weeds, watch Netflix, stalk the mail person, take the dogs on a walk, and work from the bathtub.

I feel like the chances of me losing my sight from staring at a screen and getting carpal tunnel from a mouse that is surely designed to do just that has decreased by, like, 100,000 percent (because that is a real percentage, did you know?).

Balance. It is the whipped cream to my latte, and it can be yours too.

So, back to the burrito. It's been 17 months, and I've been forced to cook far more meals than before because that goodness-wrapped-in-foil hasn't walked through my door since. But, still, I'm grateful. That burrito was just the beginning of an adventure that changed my life.

What will be your burrito? What big change will cause you to give the VA life a shot? I guarantee you, you won't regret it.

*

Finally, I'll leave you with one more small story from a VA on my team whose experience was another inspiration for writing this book. In spite of all the negative bias surrounding virtual assistants, the best VAs know their worth. They know what they're doing matters. And I wanted to end with this story because I don't think the consultant at fault meant to offend anyone. I think she just didn't know. Naivety isn't a crime, at least not in this case. But I can't wait to hand this book to her so she can see the power of VAs, of the wonderful work they can do if they're only given a chance.

Here's her story:

At a client's event this week, one of the consultants was asking me questions about what I do for work. We were having a nice, engaging conversation until she said, in front of an entire group of consultants, "Oh, so you're JUST a VA."

Honestly, I don't think she would have said it that way had she thought it through, but it came out that way as it does when we are all drinking wine. Everyone got quiet with eyes on me.

Uncomfortable was an understatement.

Once I was able to push through the weight of what she had said, I immediately went into promotion mode. I took the opportunity to tell the consultants about how fortunate I am to work with Jess and the great people at Don't Panic Management. How they take the time to know their VAs to ensure they are finding great matches for their clients—my client (whose event this was) and me being a great example.

The awkwardness ended and we carried on with the evening. But there was a part of me that wanted to scream, "Oh Mary, I am SO much more than JUST a VA!"

I'm a present mother of three and I get to be a part of every step of their growth, ensuring they have what they need to move through this world because I'm JUST a VA.

I'm the founder of an accidentally growing nonprofit that helps people realize how good they have it and makes it easy for them to pay it forward to those who aren't that fortunate because I'm JUST a VA.

I am a huge support to my husband and his goals in life and in art while still providing for my family financially because I'm JUST a VA.

Being JUST a VA has been such a great thing for me and my family. I am grateful that Jess let me stay on in the early days when things were rocky. I chose to stick with it and I am so glad I did—no matter how anyone wants to label me.

So I want to say thank you. Thank you to all the virtual assistants out there for being JUST VAs with me! I couldn't find a better group of people who inspire me with all the things you do and all the things you are inside and outside of Don't Panic Management and beyond.

appendix one

TEST PROJECT TEMPLATES, RUBRICS, AND CONTRACTS

Test Project Email Template:

We're ready to offer you your first test project on VA work. The following test is meant to evaluate your research skills, project management skills, and calendar management skills. We'll be grading you on timeliness of delivery, accuracy of the info included, formatting, and ability to follow instructions. I'm really excited about this for you, and I'm looking forward to seeing what you come up with!

Jess is working on a big push to bolster her personal brand (and, as a result, Don't Panic's). Therefore, we've been hunting for new ways to get her in front of new audiences for speaking gigs. Please research five potential speaking gigs and ten potential podcast gigs for Jess. To guide you in your search, keep in mind she speaks on content marketing, content management, outsourcing work to VAs, entrepreneurship, and what it's like to be a digital nomad and work with digital nomads.

Compile your research in a Google spreadsheet with all important data for each event or show (contact info, application deadlines, notes on the event, etc), and when it's ready for review, please share it with me.

Finally, I'll be sharing access to our task management tool, Asana, as well as Jess's speaking calendar. Please assign task reminders to Jess ("Application for X event is due today!") and calendar events (conference dates, etc) where you feel appropriate.

If you have any questions, let me know. Otherwise, please have this project completed one week from today [DATE]. The project fee for this is $75, and will be paid upon receipt of the work.

Thanks!

Here's another example test project from the social media front:

> **Project Type:** Social Media Curation
> **Fee:** $75
> **Approximate time to complete:** 3 hours
> **Project Description:** Compile one week of the Don't Panic brand's social media content. Create a calendar that includes owned and third-party content and schedule each approved social media update in Buffer. Follow up with a one-week "community management" plan.
> **Measurement:** Measure against sample created by Becca from old content.
> **Skills Tested:** Content curation, content scheduling, community management

Email Template:

We're ready to offer you a test project to track your social media skills. The following test is meant to evaluate your content curation skills, content scheduling skills, and community management skills. We'll be grading you on timeliness of delivery, accuracy of the info included, formatting, and ability to follow instructions. I'm really excited about this for you, and I'm looking forward to seeing what you come up with!

Please create a full week's worth of editorial content for the Don't Panic social media channels. Your editorial calendar should include 21 Twitter posts (3 per day), 4 Facebook posts (1 every other day), and 4 Instagram posts (1 every other day). You can read some quick and dirty advice for setting up an editorial calendar in item two of the blog post linked below.

In addition, please create a simple strategy plan (this can be a Google doc) for how you might manage an online community (say, a private Facebook group) for one week. What sort of things would you post and when? How would you get people talking to one another?

When you are finished with both items, email me for review. Once I have approved your calendar, I'll give you temporary access to our Buffer account so you can schedule the posts.

If you have any questions, let me know. Otherwise, please plan to have this project completed (including the scheduling piece) one week from today, [DATE]. The project fee for this is $75, and will be paid upon receipt of the work.

Thanks!

This one is great because it not only tests their social media abilities, but it forces them to learn more about our brand and style. For that reason, I love giving test projects that are related to internal company dealings as opposed to fake client projects. If it doesn't work out, there's no harm in (hopefully) creating a new fan of our company. If it does, the candidate is already more deeply rooted in our culture, which is a huge part of successfully retaining good people.

Test Project Rubric:

Here is a rubric we use to evaluate test projects.

Was the project turned in on time?
RED: No. [results in automatic removal from recruitment]
YELLOW: Submitted day-of, with a nudge from manager.
GREEN: Submitted on time or early.

Was it complete?
RED: No. [results in automatic removal from recruitment]
YELLOW: Required a small ping from manager (i.e., "Hey, I noticed you didn't turn in X." "OMG totally forgot to attach it to my email, so sorry! Here it is!"
GREEN: Yes!

If a process doc was provided, did they follow all steps? If not, did they follow the general instructions provided?
RED: Missed several key steps that affected the overall quality of the final delivery.
YELLOW: Missed a few small or "preferred" steps, but the end result wasn't affected.
GREEN: Yes!

Was the formatting of their final deliverable correct or thorough and usable?
RED: The formatting was messy or missing key elements (i.e., a Google sheet without a contact info column)
YELLOW: The deliverable wasn't formatted how we'd usually do it, but it's still clean and usable.
GREEN: The deliverable was formatted the way we would have done it ourselves.

Was the information inside the deliverable accurate?

RED: No. Important pieces of information were either missing or incorrect.

YELLOW: For the most part, yes, but a few "expert level" pieces of knowledge were missing.

GREEN: All information was complete and accurate to the best of our knowledge.

Did the project require major edits for tone, grammar, or punctuation?

RED: Yes. Assignment needed a complete language overhaul or major edits.

YELLOW: There were a few noticeable typos or structure issues, but the meat was fine.

GREEN: The project required minor edits or no changes at all.

How did it measure against the sample assignment?

RED: Totally missed the mark.

YELLOW: Not quite as strong, but still a useful deliverable.

GREEN: As good or better than the sample assignment.

Finally, if this assignment were being delivered to a real client, could it be submitted as-is or with minimal editing?

RED: Not a chance in hell.

YELLOW: If it were run through our client manager's editing process, it would be good to go.

GREEN: You bet! Client manager would feel comfortable delivering work product without further review.

FINAL SCORE: _____ / 3

Reds are worth 1 point, Yellows are worth 2, Greens are worth 3. Add it up and collect the average (divide by 8). Tester must average a 2.5 or higher to be considered eligible to move forward.

Contracts:

Visit http://dontpanicmgmt.com/sample-contract to download an up-to-date sample of a VA contract that you can use in your own business.

appendix two

TOOLS OF THE TRADE

Here's the long list of virtual tools to keep in mind, along with a description and list of pros and cons of the ones that I personally use at Don't Panic Management. It's a bit of a doozy, so if you see one you like, try it! Worst case scenario, it doesn't work for you and you can move on to the next one.

For a full, up-to-date list of tools we use in our daily lives at Don't Panic, visit:
http://dontpanicmgmt.com/va-tools

Note: These tools are not affiliates and I don't get any sort of benefit—monetary or otherwise—for recommending them.

Meetings & Communications

Zoom https://zoom.us/

In the world of online meeting software, Zoom is relatively new to the playing field. They're a popular option these days because they offer a free option as well as a paid plan that's more affordable than some of the enterprise options, like GoToMeeting.

Zoom was made to be a video conferencing solution, so that's what they do best, but the tool can also be used for webinars and trainings for up to 500 video participants and 10,000 viewers.

For video conferences, I have found Zoom to be the most reliable option. It's easy for users to access and doesn't seem to drop the connection as frequently as other providers. It also has a recording function with paid plans, which is especially useful for people who can't join a meeting or who would like to re-watch an important training, for example.

Pros:

- Reliable, stable video conferencing solution
- Many feature options and plans to accommodate different business needs
- Recording capability
- Instant message and file-sharing

Cons:

- Free plan has limited features, so you really need to pay for this tool to get the full benefit

Cost: Free to host up to 100 participants and unlimited 1:1 meetings. Free version does not include recording feature. Pro plans start at $14.99 per month per host. Business plans start at $19.99 per month per host.

Uberconference https://www.uberconference.com/

Uberconference is a simple, no frills audio conference solution for teams of all sizes. Its free solution is good enough for most meeting needs. It also allows for call recording and screen sharing so you can use it for things like trainings. Uberconference does not have a video conferencing option and is not always reliable, which is why we moved to a Zoom account and currently use Uberconference as our secondary conferencing tool.

Pros:

- Easy access via phone or browser
- Audio and screen sharing controls
- Includes chat functionality
- Customizable hold music (we use Rick Astley's *Never Gonna Give You Up*)
- Automatic recording

Cons:

- No video option
- Frequent bugs (at least on free plan) that

sometimes prevent users from hearing each other on the browser version

Cost: Free for up to 10 participants. The Business plan is $10 per line so you can set up different lines for different teams or departments. These lines can host up to 100 participants, allow for international access, have the option to dial out to add guests to a call, enable you to create your own custom hold music, and much more.

Skype https://www.skype.com/

To me, Skype is the "original" VoIP calling solution. I remember studying abroad in college and using it to call my friends and family back home. When I got a webcam, it was the tool I used to share video as well. As a result, Skype is still one of the most common, quick ways to connect with someone online. I don't want to spend too much time on it, though, because it doesn't offer a lot of the business features that many other conferencing and communications platforms do. I just, you know, couldn't make a section of communications tools without including our dear old Skype!

Pros:

- Easy download and sign-up process
- Free to make video and audio calls
- Includes chat functionality
- Ability to add multiple participants
- Includes screen sharing functionality
- Allows phone calls for a fee

Cons:

- Not always reliable
- Does not allow recording without a third-party add-on

Cost: Free for Skype-to-Skype calling. Nominal per-minute fees for making calls to cell phones or landlines.

Sococo http://sococo.com/

(Full Disclosure: Sococo is a former client, but we started using the tool BEFORE they became a client so I believe this is an unbiased review.)

Sococo quite literally changed the way we do business at Don't Panic. Let me explain. Sococo is essentially a virtual office environment unlike anything I've ever seen before. It allows you to set up what looks like a two-dimensional office space, cubicles and all, and assign spaces to each of your team members. When you get suited up for work each day, you log into your Sococo office and your little "Bob" avatar shows up as online and available in your "office."

As a manager, it's great to see when your various team members are online and working, especially when you run a virtual company that has people in different locations and across time zones. We don't require certain working hours and we like to respect people's boundaries, so using the "available in Sococo" cue is great for knowing when we can bother someone with questions or ramblings (which I do to my team quite frequently).

It's also a great way to hold meetings, whether they're audio or video, seamlessly. We can meet in whatever room we choose and we can also invite external guests, even if they're not a part of our Sococo team. We simply send them a link and they can click it to be placed in our meeting room.

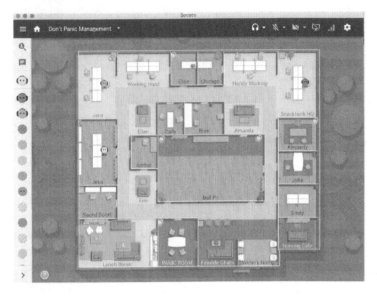

(It's early in the day as I'm taking this screenshot . . . it's not always this much of a ghost town!)

Sococo is a little finicky and it doesn't always work for guests. Guests need to have the latest version of Chrome, for example, and they need to be able to figure out where the audio controls are. Even then, sometimes their browser or computer doesn't like to recognize the tool, so then they can't hear us or see us (and vice versa).

This instability and unreliability has caused us to adopt Zoom as a backup so we don't need to worry about troubleshooting with every new business call we take, but we truly love Sococo for the way it's brought our own team closer together with ease. Plus, it has a mobile app for when I'm on a road trip in the middle of nowhere but need to hop on a standup meeting with my favorite ladies. The mobile app isn't perfect and doesn't support video or screen sharing like the desktop version, but it works for audio just fine.

Pros:

- Unlike any other communications tool in that it gives everyone an "office"
- Allows users to set away, available, and busy status updates
- Includes chat, video calls, audio calls, and screen sharing options
- Customizable office layouts and colors to let you show your personality
- Responsive customer service (for all the various bug issues, which I mention below)
- Separate desktop and mobile app
- Desktop notifications ping you when your attention is needed, but you can customize which notifications you want to see (such as new messages to you, but not when someone signs on or off)

Cons:

- Frequent updates cause some instability in the product
- Frequent bugs occur as a result of frequent updates (for example, sometimes we get

randomly logged out, can't hear each other, or have connection problems)
- Requires a bit of a learning curve to figure out how it works
- Mobile app does not support all features of the desktop/browser app

Cost: Free for a 30-day trial, then free for small teams (up to 10 members with limited features) or $15 per member for the full monty.

Slack https://slack.com/

Slack's adorable ads with all the zoo animals working together really tugged on my heartstrings when I first saw them. That's because they're a company that truly believes in the power of the virtual workforce. As a result, they've built a tool that allows teams to communicate effectively, wherever and whenever they want. Many of our clients use Slack as their primary communication channel, even more than email, which at first was surprising to me, but then I understood.

The way you can thread conversations, attach files, and separate different conversations and teams with Channels makes it almost like a project management tool and a communications tool combined. Their mobile app is very slick and their desktop app let you know when you're needed in a conversation even if you don't have the app open. Super useful, especially when you need quick answers to a question or need to keep a group looped in on a project.

Slack saves communications as well and those messages are searchable, so if you need to go looking for something you talked about last month, well, voila!

No one needs more emails and Slack is a great option for real-time, organized communication that you can take on the go.

Pros:

- Easy, intuitive, and streamlined communication for the whole team
- Desktop notifications so you know when you're needed
- Beautiful mobile app to communicate on the go
- Integrates with nearly every productivity and project management tool out there (or you can build your own integration with their open API)
- Includes one-on-one voice and video calls with the free plan and one-on-one or team (up to 15 people) voice and video calls, including screen sharing, with paid plans

Cons:

- For me, the only con is the user interface. It's simple, but not beautiful. I personally prefer Sococo's chat and availability functions combined with Asana's task manager interface. But that's a personal preference thing! I hear only good things from colleagues who use Slack on a daily, if not hourly, basis.

Cost: Free for small teams with limited features. $8 per user per month for the "standard" plan and $15 per user per month for the "plus" plan.

Google Hangouts https://hangouts.google.com/

Every time you make a calendar invitation through Google Calendars, a Google Hangout link gets added by default (unless you turn off this setting in the admin panel). Therefore, it has become a go-to resource for many businesses that use Google to manage their email, files, and calendar.

I don't find anything inherently wrong with Google Hangouts. With one click, it's an easy way to get teams together on a video chat. The issue that irks me though is the amount of bandwidth it takes to run the video. I find that when I'm on a Google Hangout, my computer doesn't like to let me do anything else. I don't find this to be the case with Zoom, which also allows for video conferencing. At some point, it's all about preference here. Google Hangouts can be inserted automatically into calendar invitations whereas Zoom details need to be pasted in, for example, and not everyone wants to go through the hassle of pasting details. I get it.

Google Hangouts can also be used as a live broadcasting tool which is appealing from a marketing perspective. You can schedule a Hangout and guests can see it live or view the recorded version after the fact if you wish to make it available. There are lots of interesting use cases for this facet of the tool.

Pros:

- Easy, one-click video web conferencing tool
- Allows for screen sharing, audio, video, and text chat options
- Ability to schedule meetings and broadcast live to YouTube

Cons:

- Requires a lot of bandwidth
- Can be glitchy with hearing and seeing other participants
- Gets added automatically to Google Calendar invitations unless you remember turn off that feature, which can be confusing to guests
- No local recording option

Cost: Free.

Loom: https://www.useloom.com/

I don't know what I was doing before I found Loom. Loom provides the simplest, easiest way to shoot a quick video for someone. It includes your face in the corner and a screencast of whatever you want on your desktop. You get the screencast element that other tools, like Jive, provide while including the personalization element of having a video of you as well.

When you've completed a video, you don't have to be burdened by downloading it to your computer and then uploading it to send. Those video files can be giant, which is a huge hassle (ha, literally). Loom simply lets you share the video as a link. When someone clicks on it, you get notified so you can tell when someone watches. Creepy, perhaps, but also useful!

Loom makes it easy to record and send videos directly inside Gmail with a click, instead of copying the link, opening your email, and pasting it. Viewers can then view the videos directly in their email inbox. This may not be a big time saver when you're recording a one-off, but if you're creating these kinds of videos consistently, that copy, paste, open, and click time will add up.

Take whatever shortcuts you can get as long as you're not actually shortcutting when it comes to doing great business.

Did I mention that all of this is free? At this point, all Loom wants are referrals. Without a referral, you can shoot videos that are only 10 minutes maximum. But after you refer one person (again, to use this FREE service), you get to record videos with unlimited time.

If you couldn't tell, I love this tool. Sometimes I shoot a quick Loom in place of an email. Or I use it to show someone something without scheduling a meeting. It has saved me crazy amounts of time and frustration.

Pros:

- Chrome browser extension
- Easy to install and use
- Link-sharing capability as opposed to downloading video files

- Save and categorize your videos inside your account
- Facebook and Twitter share links
- HTML embed for websites
- Comments allowed
- Free!

Cons:

- 10-minute limit on videos (prior to successful referral)
- Relatively new tool, so you never know how long it will last

Cost: Free, with an option to upgrade for pro features (which at the time of writing, do not exist).

GoVideo https://www.vidyard.com/govideo/

After I started using Loom, I learned that Vidyard has a similar tool that was originally called ViewedIt and is now called GoVideo. It's extremely similar in functionality to Loom, so as far as I'm concerned, you could use either one interchangeably.

One thing that GoVideo features is a more prominent Gmail and social media integration. GoVideo seems to be positioned as more of a business and sales tool than an internal sharing tool, allowing you to track views and follow up with viewers afterwards.

Pros:

- Chrome browser extension

- Easy to install and use
- Link-sharing capability vs. downloading video files
- Gmail integration
- Save and categorize videos inside your account
- Gmail, YouTube, Facebook, LinkedIn, and Twitter integration for easier sharing
- Lead/view tracker for easy follow up
- Free!

Cons:

- 1-hour recording limit
- Cannot download videos
- Comments not allowed except for on social/email

Cost: Free.

Other communications tools to try:

- Hipchat
- Join Me
- GoToMeeting

Calendar & Scheduling

Google Calendar https://calendar.google.com/

At Don't Panic Management, we live and die by all things Google (except for Google Hangouts!), so this was the natural first recommendation for a calendaring platform. If you have Google Apps set up for your business (that means email, Drive, etc.) then Google

Calendar is the obvious choice because it's already integrated in what you're doing with your email. Also, it's a very common calendaring tool so most VAs already know how to use it.

Many of the other tools I use have an integration with Google Calendar which increases its value. It has an intuitive platform and is very reliable, which is why I use it.

Pros:

- Clean user interface and easy to set up with any Google account
- Easy to add new events and meeting attendees
- Color-coding and customization options make it clear which events are which
- Sharing features allow other team members to view, edit, and change events
- Available/busy times make it clear what your status is
- New "block" feature lets you select times where people can schedule meetings with you and share those out (similar to a Calendly or MixMax functionality)
- Slick mobile app

Cons:

- None

Cost: Free for Gmail users and included with GSuite business plans.

Calendly https://calendly.com/

Calendly allows you to integrate your calendars and then create different "events" that you can share for easy meeting scheduling. You can set preferred meeting times or let guests pick any time that's free on your calendar. The tool will look at the calendars you've integrated to make sure guests can only see times that are not already booked.

Once guests pick a time on your calendar, they receive an automated confirmation email that has the details to join the meeting, which you can set manually. For example, we always like to use our Zoom conference line for new business meetings, so the Zoom details automatically get sent to the guest who will be joining the meeting.

Then, I receive an email confirmation that someone has just scheduled a meeting with me and it automatically shows up on my Google calendar. If someone needs to cancel or reschedule, they can do so directly from the confirmation email or calendar invitation.

You can customize the automatic responses when you pay for a plan, but with their free plan you are tied to their existing templates.

Pros:

- Easy to setup and integrate with calendars
- Separate links for separate events (such as new business request, operations consulting session, discovery call, etc.)
- Automatic calendar events and confirmations

- Easy rescheduling/canceling options
- Easy for meeting guests to navigate
- Customization of meeting location and details
- Affordable paid plans for many, many more useful features
- Over 700 app integrations with the paid plans

Cons:

- No direct Gmail integration
- Not many features included in the free plan
- No mobile app

Cost: Free for limited features, otherwise $8-$12 per user per month depending on the types of features you need.

Doodle https://doodle.com/

If you have a group of people that you're trying to schedule something with, whether it be a bachelorette party or a marketing brainstorm meeting, Doodle offers a great solution. The creator of the Doodle can select multiple dates and times for people to choose from and then send out a link to the poll. Once attendees fill out the Doodle, it will highlight the times that all (or the majority of) attendees can make so that you can easily pick the best one. This makes wrangling tough schedules much, much easier!

Pros:

- Easy setup
- No need for attendees to create an account

- Free for basic features
- Simple polling option for scheduling meetings with multiple guests
- Includes calendar integration
- Mobile app

Cons:

- None!

Cost: Free for basic features, then $39-$69 per year for more advanced features, such as custom design, removal of ads, additional guest information, and custom subdomains.

MixMax https://mixmax.com/

I only recently heard of MixMax and I'm glad I did because it's a nifty solution to picking meeting times that work for your guests in a visually appealing way. Its built-in Gmail integration allows you to simply click the extension from within an email, drag times across your calendar, and embed those calendar options directly into the email itself. This allows guests to pick a meeting time from your list of options instead of going back and forth about who's available when.

This scheduling tool almost replaces the need for a scheduling assistant! But I'd argue it's best to have your VA do the sending of MixMax meeting times. Even though it only takes a few minutes, those minutes add up when you're scheduling a lot of meetings.

MixMax was built as a sales tool, so it also includes features like scheduling emails, seeing who has read your emails, sales templates, and much more.

Pros:

- Easy, clean installation and user interface
- Integrates with Gmail and Salesforce
- Includes analytics
- Integrates with calendar for easy scheduling

Cons:

- Not free, but otherwise I haven't had any issues with this tool

Cost: $9 per user per month for the starter package and up to $49 per use per month for additional features.

Productivity

Pomodoro Timer

Have you ever heard of the Pomodoro method for getting things done? It works like this:

Work without interruption for 25 minutes and then get a 5-minute break. This is considered one Pomodoro. After four Pomodoros, or approximately two hours, you get a longer break. This break is usually fifteen to thirty minutes, depending on how you're feeling.

By providing time for hard work and time for frequent breaks, I've found this technique to be extremely helpful when I need to get difficult or time-consuming projects done. I'm always surprised at how much I can do in the 25-minute sprints and then how great the 5-minute breaks are for checking email and social media.

You can use this technique with a regular timer and piece of paper, or you can use a desktop or mobile app to help you track the time. I use the Tomighty app for my Mac (http://tomighty.org) because it's free, easy to install, and has a toolbar icon that I can find and click when I'm ready to start my Pomodoros.

There are tons of apps and tools out there so I encourage you to try a free one first and then upgrade to a paid tool if you want more features and tracking options.

Harvest Time Tracking https://www.getharvest.com/

Harvest is a common, easy-to-use time tracking tool. This is useful if you work in an agency environment and bill hourly like we do. It integrates with several other tools we use, such as Asana, so you can track time against a specific task or project. It's very straightforward and very affordable for small businesses. Many of our clients use Harvest not only for tracking their time, but also for invoicing their clients and tallying expenses. They are able to provide their hourly, tracked reports inside of each invoice, which is extremely useful for everyone.

Harvest integrates with all kinds of other tools and apps, including Asana, Trello, Basecamp, Quickbooks, Paypal, Slack, and many more.

Pros:

- Easy invoicing, expense-tracking, and time-tracking software
- Affordable solution for businesses of all sizes
- Mobile and desktop apps available
- Chrome and Safari plugin for time tracking
- Monitor team time to compare with project estimates

Cons:

- Does not include as many features as a tool like Quickbooks, so can't necessarily replace a full-scale accounting tool

Cost: Free for individuals with up to two projects. After that, it's $12 per person per month for unlimited projects.

Boomerang https://www.boomeranggmail.com/

I haven't found another tool quite like Boomerang. It's an email plugin that allows you to schedule emails, track follow ups, and remind you when someone hasn't responded to your emails in a certain number of days.

I'm the kind of person who likes to set it and forget it, so sometimes when I send an email asking for feedback or some kind of information, I tend to think my job is done. Well, we all know that's not the case if you don't receive a response! Boomerang shoots that email back to the top of my inbox when I haven't heard anything for a day, a week, a month, or however long I choose.

That way, I am reminded to follow up with that person with another email or a phone call.

It's great for me because I don't have to remember to remember to follow up!

Another great benefit of Boomerang is the scheduling feature. I often work late nights and weekends, but I don't necessarily want my clients or colleagues to know that. I can schedule emails for the following morning or Monday during normal business hours and shazam! I get to protect my schedule and still work on my own time.

Pros:

- One-click install to Gmail using the plugin
- Easy email scheduling
- "Boomerang" emails back to your inbox when people haven't responded
- Move emails to an archive folder until you need them
- Mobile app
- Includes other tools, such as Respondable to help you craft the perfect email and Inbox Pause to help you be more productive

Cons:

- Only works with Gmail and Outlook
- Does not work if you use a third party email tool to manage your Gmail

Cost: Free for basic features. Personal, Pro, and Premium accounts are between $4.99 and $49.99 per month.

Other productivity apps to use:

- IFTTT
- Zapier

Project & Task Management

Asana https://asana.com

After using a tool called Samepage for over a year, we recently switched to Asana for all of our project and task management needs. Asana is a great starter option for anyone looking to try a project management tool because it doesn't have the unnecessary bells and whistles that a lot of the more robust options have.

We needed a place to store projects and files, invite people to collaborate, and integrate with our favorite tools like Gmail and Loom. Asana fit the bill for us and has been working really well for the last several months.

I personally love the email reminders when tasks are due, the ability to reply to tasks and mark them complete from an email reply, and the daily recap of what's coming up. The only feature I wish Asana had was a desktop app. I love to keep anything that's not an article out of my browser whenever possible because I am a tab-hoarder and things tend get lost that way. Hopefully the Asana team is working on building a desktop app as we speak!

Pros:

- Easy project and task management system
- Permissions options to keep certain files and projects secure
- Unlimited tasks, projects, and conversations
- Data security and backup features
- Free for small teams
- Filtering options to see tasks and projects as you wish
- No fluff, no frills
- Calendar and Gmail integration
- Harvest integration
- Loom integration
- Mobile app

Cons:

- No desktop app

Cost: Free for up to 15 team members. Premium account is $9.99 per user per month and allows for more advanced features such as advanced search and reporting, private teams and projects, and start dates for ongoing or long-term projects.

Other project management tools to try:

- Basecamp
- Workfront
- Teamwork
- Trello
- Ontraport
- SamePage

File Sharing & Collaboration

Dropbox https://www.dropbox.com/

Dropbox is a common file-sharing tool for businesses both large and small. It is a secure way to host all types of files in the cloud. We have the 1TB plan, which works well because we produce a lot of podcasts that take up a *lot* of space. With folders for each client and different sharing permissions for each folder, we are able to easily organize and access what we need to get our work done. Dropbox's newer Paper feature allows you to work collaboratively on a document, similar to how Google Drive works, and be notified of comments via email.

Pros:

- Many businesses and individuals have already adopted this tool, so this one is easy to integrate
- Desktop and mobile apps allow you to read, view, and edit documents directly from your computer or mobile device
- Share entire folders or individuals files with a link
- Comment and work collaboratively on documents
- Basic plan is free
- File recovery system if a folder or file is accidentally deleted

Cons:

- Can get expensive if you work with a larger team and need a lot of cloud storage space

Cost: Free for Basic individual plan (2 GB) and up from there. The Plus plan for individuals is $9.99 per month for 1TB of storage space. For businesses, the Standard plan is $12.50 per user per month, starting at three users.

Google Drive https://drive.google.com/

If you're a Gmail freak like I am, Google Drive is a natural solution for file storage and sharing. For the most part, we store collaborative spreadsheets and documents in Google Drive folders, but use Dropbox for bigger files like podcasts and videos. If a client prefers one tool over another, we go ahead and use their tool of choice exclusively.

As far as functionality, the commenting, sharing, and collaborative nature of Google Drive is unmatched, especially as a free tool.

Pros:

- Collaborative document creation and editing tool that can be used with or without a Google account
- Tag people in comments to assign tasks
- Mobile and desktop app
- Offline editing feature
- Integrates with Gmail

Cons:

- Not everyone likes the Google Drive interface, so the search for the perfect collaboration and storage tool continues

Cost: Free for up to 15GB of space. $1.99 per month for 100GB, $9.99 per month for 1TB, and $99.99 per month for 10TB.

Other file sharing & collaboration tools to try:

- Box
- SharePoint
- Evernote

Travel Booking

Google Flights https://www.google.com/flights/

You're probably sensing a theme with all these Google recommendations by now. I just can't help myself! Google Flights is another great service from the media giant. It allows you to search different airline sites at once for the best flight time, price, and airline. It's a useful way for anyone, but especially VAs, to find options for busy client travel schedules. Once you've found the flight option you like, you can click through to the purchase page the way you'd buy any other flight.

Pros:

- Easy comparison of flights across airlines
- Filtering allows you to pick the best times, durations, and costs
- Easy booking through the provider of your choice, including Expedia and Orbitz
- Set up alerts to track prices
- Book directly through Google on some itineraries

- Share itineraries with friends and family before booking

Cons:

- Does not look at certain airlines, such as Southwest Airlines

Cost: Free.

Kayak https://www.kayak.com/

Kayak is so similar to Google Flights that I won't go into too much detail with it, but I will say that Kayak also includes the same kind of search functionality for hotels, car rentals, and vacation packages. Kayak compares results from other travel sites like Expedia, Priceline, and Orbitz so you can pick the best deal.

Pros:

- Easy travel comparison search engine for flights, hotels, car rentals, and vacation packages
- Compares with other popular travel search engines
- Book directly through Kayak or through your chosen booking site
- Easy filtering options for price, number of stops, vendors

Cons:

- Does not look at certain airlines, such as Southwest Airlines

Cost: Free.

HotelTonight https://www.hoteltonight.com/

This tool is all about what the name says: Finding a hotel tonight! This is especially useful for last-minute trips and for finding deals in big cities like New York. When hotels have leftover rooms that they want to sell at the last minute, they'll often post discounts to apps like this one. You cannot request certain types of rooms or floors, so there's a chance you won't get the room you wanted. This is the tradeoff for booking a cheap, last-minute room. HotelTonight can show you rooms up to one week out from your travel date.

Pros:

- Best prices on last-minute hotel bookings
- No hidden fees to the app
- Easy viewing of rooms, locations, and rates
- Easy booking

Cons:

- Cannot select room type (but you can make requests in the comments that may or may not be honored by the hotel)
- Not available everywhere

Cost: Free.

TripIt https://www.tripit.com/

TripIt is my favorite travel organization tool besides Google Calendar. When you sign up for an account, you can set up an email integration that allows you to simply forward travel plan confirmation emails to plans@tripit.com. They will automatically be set up as an itinerary in TripIt. Your TripIt calendar feed can then be integrated to your Google Calendar, so you can see all of your flight, hotel, car, and restaurant reservation details directly in line with whatever other calendar events you've set up. Like magic!

Pros:

- Easy way to collect all of your travel plans in one place
- Email integration so you can forward plans and have them be organized automatically
- Calendar integration
- Automatically detects conflicts in plans
- Pro version tracks flight delays, cancellations, and other trip issues
- Teams account for sharing plans and collaborating with different users
- Concur integration for expense tracking and reporting

Cons:

- Many of the best features are not included in the free version, but if you're a big traveler, the Pro version is worthwhile

Cost: Free for the basic version and $49 per year for the Pro version.

Security

LastPass https://www.lastpass.com/

There's nothing scarier than sharing your personal data with someone you don't know. I get that. That's why I always recommend using a secure tool that you control to share passwords, credit card information, and other private data. LastPass is my tool of choice, however there are a lot of other tools that offer similar functionality so it's important to pick the one you feel most comfortable with.

The way it works is that you can add secure items one by one, such as logins or credit card data, and then share them with your team. When you share, you have the option of allowing the team member to see the password or hiding it. When they create an account and accept your share items, they can install the browser plugin and be able to use your logins seamlessly. That way, they can get into your accounts with or without password viewing access. If for any reason you let go of or lose a team member, you can revoke their access to the items and they will no longer be able to access them. They also won't be able to take the logins with them if you prevent them from viewing the passwords. It's a great way to keep your information safe and secure.

Pros:

- Secure data storage that can be shared across teams
- Store logins, credit card information, or other secure notes
- Choose permissions on each shared item or folder
- Easily remove access and accounts if team status changes

Cons:

- Cannot use without a LastPass account
- The autofill feature can be finicky and if you have access to a lot of logins, you may find yourself logging into the wrong account if you're not careful

Cost: Personal and family accounts are $2-$4 per month. Business accounts are $2.42-$4 per user per month as well, but provide more features than the personal and family accounts.

Other security tools to try:

- Dead Drop
- 1Password

Podcasting

Zencastr https://zencastr.com/

Zencastr is my tool of choice for recording podcast episodes with remote co-hosts and/or guests. It's a web application that allows you to easily create a link for guests to join without downloading any software or creating any sort of account. As the admin, you have controls for recording, mixing, adding effects, and much more during the recording. Or, you can simply hit record and let your assistant do all the production work after the recording is finished!

The tool connects to your Dropbox account and recordings are automatically saved there once you end the recording and everyone's audio track has uploaded. If it's a clean recording, you can also click the "automatic postproduction" button and have the tracks mixed together for you. It's easy and affordable, especially for beginning podcasters.

Pros:

- VoIP web application that works with Chrome and Firefox browsers
- No installation of software required to use the tool
- Admin needs an account to save recordings but guests don't need an account to join a recording
- Separate tracks for each guest (so if you get a doorbell, a dog barking, or a child screaming at someone's home office, you can edit it out easily without compromising the other audio tracks)

- High quality MP3 output
- Record up to three hours in one session

Cons:

- Does not work on mobile (yet)
- Free plan allows up to two guests only
- Relatively new tool, so there are some technical glitches from time to time

Cost: The Hobbyist plan is free, but only allows up to two guests and eight hours of recording per month. The Professional plan is great for most podcasters and allows unlimited guests, unlimited recordings, high quality mp3 and wav files, and ten hours of automatic postproduction per month.

Rev https://www.rev.com/

At Don't Panic Management, we've been asked to do transcriptions many times, but we always recommend a tool like Rev instead. Rev is affordable at just $1 per minute and they also provide captioning services for the same fee. Their YouTube integration is great if you've published a video and then want to have timed captions included. They'll transcribe the video, create the caption file, and deliver it directly back to YouTube for you. In my experience, their transcription and caption services usually take a matter of hours, depending on how long the initial file is. If you're using the transcriptions or captions for anything besides your own personal needs, you'll need to review carefully to check for typos, but for the most part they're pretty accurate.

Pros:

- Fast, easy, and affordable transcription service
- Video integration allows you to caption published videos
- Timely and helpful support
- Fast turnaround
- Useful for transcribing interviews, speeches, and podcast episodes

Cons:

- Occasional typos or misunderstanding of proper nouns and certain phrases

Cost: $1 per minute for transcription and captioning services. Translation services cost a bit more.

Libsyn https://www.libsyn.com/

Libsyn is the most popular media storage tool for podcasters. Once you've got your show details set up, you're given a feed that you can submit to every popular podcasting platform, including iTunes, Stitcher, Google Play, Overcast, and more. It also integrates with other apps like Spotify and IHeartRadio so you can get your show in front of more audiences. The plans are affordable depending on how much storage you need and whether you're interested in your podcast's statistics or not.

Pros:

- Easy setup and configuration of podcasts
- Provides a feed to submit to podcast platforms

- Includes an embeddable media player
- Basic or advanced statistics depending on your plan
- No-frills solution to media storage and hosting

Cons:

- A little clunky to use and can be counterintuitive to figure out at first . . . but you get used to it!

Cost: $5-$75 per month depending on how many megabytes you need and what level of statistics you're interested in. The most common plan that we use is the $15 per month plan, which gets you 250mb of storage and includes basic statistics.

Other podcasting tools to try:

- GarageBand
- Audacity
- Skype
- iMovie
- Final Cut Pro
- Ringr
- Wavve
- Auphonic

Social Media Management

Buffer https://buffer.com/

Pretty much all social media channels come with some form of analytics or insights for business accounts and pages, but they aren't always particularly robust. Buffer offers a scheduling tool that lets you plan and draft content ahead of time (so you can automate some of those workflows, yo!). Their in-depth reporting that tracks a number of KPIs is just the icing on the cake.

Pros:

- Super easy-to-use interface
- Manage many accounts across multiple brands
- Invite team members to your channels so you can collaborate on content
- You can pause your entire queue (a savvy capability in a crisis)
- Use the Buffer browser extension to make content curation a breeze
- Choose a recurring content schedule or publish posts on the fly

Cons:

- Not all that awesome stuff comes for free—the best features for a small business or social media manager (like the analytics) exist on the paid plans only
- Some newer social media networks can't be automated through Buffer (What up, SnapChat!)

Cost: Individual accounts range from free to $10 per month. Team and agency accounts range from $99-$399 per month. To get the most useful features, you'll probably at least want to opt for the $99 per month Small Business plan.

Buzzsumo http://buzzsumo.com/

Buzzsumo is the Buzz-bomb-o. (It's not a good joke, I know, but this is an appendix. I'm trying to make it a little more interesting for you.) Buzzsumo helps you align your content strategy by making it possible to search a topic or domain and see what content is performing best under that domain or term. It can also help you identify influencers who can help you promote your content.

For example, the top shared pieces of content for "virtual assistant" right now are articles about how Morgan Freeman voiced Mark Zuckerberg's personal home assistant. Sigh. For the last time, people, Siri and Alexa are NOT VAs!

Pros:

- Filter your results by a variety of time periods so you can see what is trending today, this week, this year, and more
- Results share information about engagements, backlinks, trending topics—the list goes on
- The domain feature makes it possible to see what kinds of content are performing well for your competitors
- The advanced search features rock! Search by type of content, word count, and more.
- There's a "micro" plan for solopreneurs and freelancers
- Set up content alerts for terms or domains of particular interest

Cons:

- Free access to Buzzsumo gets you very little. You'll have to pay if you really want to make this tool work for you.

Cost: Monthly plans range from $99-$499 monthly, but you can save 20% if you pay your invoices annually instead. The micro plan is more affordable (just $39 per month), but you have to apply for access.

Canva https://www.canva.com/

Canva is basically a browser-based graphics designer for dummies. Use the relatively simple tools and templates to put together gorgeous blog graphics, social media images, flyers, and even resumes. This tool is awesome because it allows graphically challenged folks (like me) to create something more professional without buying expensive illustration software.

Pros:

- The image templates come optimized by type— no guessing what the best size is for a blog post v. Facebook
- Canva can auto-convert designs into different templates, making repurposing images for different social media channels easy
- Sort designs into folders so you can separate projects by brands or type
- Plenty of storage (at least 1GB on all plans)
- Specially priced plans for teachers and nonprofits

Cons:

- It can sometimes be a little clunky to use
- Some of the cooler templates and designs are paid only

Cost: A basic version of the tool is free. Most of the features listed above are part of the "Canva for Work" plan: $12.95 per user per month. Save 23% when you sign up for a yearly plan.

Other social media tools to try:

- Tweetdeck
- SocialRank
- Moz
- Hootsuite
- Agorapulse

Content Management

WordPress https://wordpress.org/

WordPress is the most popular website hosting and content management tool because it's got hundreds of thousands of themes to choose from and is easy for even the most technologically un-savvy user to figure out. I won't go too deep into this one because chances are you've already heard of it and use it yourself!

Pros:

- Easy, one-click installation that integrates with most popular hosting platforms
- Thousands of free and paid themes so you don't have to hire a developer
- Thousands of free and paid plugins available to increase functionality
- Intuitive backend for publishing content
- Integration with many popular tools
- Mobile app
- Open source software, so contributors are always working to make it better

Cons:

- Not everyone finds this tool to be as easy to use as I do
- Too many plugins can slow the site way down
- Your options are limited if you're not working with a developer and don't have coding knowledge

Cost: Free to download, but themes, plugins, and hosting usually cost money.

CoSchedule https://coschedule.com/

CoSchedule is easily my favorite content management tool on the planet. And they didn't have to pay me to say that, I swear. I love how easy it is to map all kinds of content types on one calendar, color code them, and schedule associated social media shares. The tool integrates with your blog so you can see exactly which content is being published when. It also includes a workflow system where you can assign tasks, tag people in comments, set due dates, and use templates for everyone involved in each content project. This tool has saved my life on more than one occasion and I can't recommend it highly enough for anyone who is looking for a simple solution to content marketing management.

Pros:

- Manage all of your content in one place, from blog posts to emails, podcasts to social media, and everything in between
- Color-coding
- Task management for projects that involve multiple team members
- Workflow templates for any and all content projects
- Great blog content and customer support

Cons:

- Not free, and many of the best features are available only in the more expensive plans

Cost: Starting at $40 per month for individual accounts and up to $2,200 for corporate accounts. They also have an agency option which is awesome if you manage multiple calendars and clients.

Rainmaker
https://rainmakerdigital.com/about/technology/

When we were deciding where to go with our new Don't Panic Management website last year, we were drawn to Rainmaker for a number of reasons. First, it's got many of the functionality that plugins provide already built in. For example, a course-making option, a product-selling option, and a membership option. While we weren't sure exactly how the company would grow, we knew that these features may become relevant over time. Rainmaker was created by the folks over at Copyblogger (hi, friends!) and has a great support team on board for every silly question or concern. They also have a list of recommended developers who are well-versed in the platform, so you can choose someone trustworthy to build and maintain your site. Plus, the backend is very similar to WordPress so the learning curve isn't too steep for the average content or website manager. For all of these reasons, we switched to Rainmaker for our 2016 redesign.

Pros:

- Built-in features, such as courses, memberships, and products
- Similar backend to WordPress
- Great support
- Vetted team of trusted developers
- Fast and secure
- Mobile-friendly

Cons:

- The Rainmaker Platform is no longer available as a standalone service and I'm so sorry to hear this!

Cost: The Rainmaker Platform is now part of Rainmaker Digital, so you must get in touch with the Rainmaker Digital folks to set up a demo.

Grammarly https://www.grammarly.com/

No one is perfect and typos are bound to happen. You probably found a few in this book, despite the fact that I used robot and human editors alike. But Grammarly is here to rescue you and your typo-ridden fingers. This free browser plugin looks at all of the copy you're creating and highlights issues, whether they're in an email, a Google Doc, or a blog post. It's super useful for pointing out some of those grammar faux pas that you may not readily notice, such as passive sentences, missing (or extra) commas, and word usage issues. Instead of only focusing on the red-underlined spelling mistakes, let Grammarly make you a better writer.

Pros:

- Browser plugin allows you to see grammar mistakes and issues across web content
- Easy to install and use
- Reject or approve grammar suggestions with a click of a button
- Free to use
- Desktop app available for non-browser documents

Cons:

- Sometimes suggestions are not relevant
- Doesn't always know proper nouns or certain phrases

Cost: Free for a basic account, which includes basic grammar and spelling highlights. The Premium version costs $29.95 per month and includes advanced features like plagiarism checks and style-specific suggestions.

Other content management tools to try:

- Squarespace
- Kapost
- DivvyHQ
- Hubspot

Email Marketing

ConvertKit https://convertkit.com/

ConvertKit, as I write this, is my email marketing tool of choice. In addition to providing easy segmentation and tagging options for subscribers, ConvertKit allows you to create landing pages for email collection that can either stand on their own or be embedded on a website. Most of the small-business-focused email marketing tools do not allow this, so this is a great feature if you don't want to pay for a separate landing page tool like LeadPages.

ConvertKit has drag-and-drop templates, one-click "send to unopens", and other easy, intuitive features that has caused me to ditch Mailchimp. Its price point is competitive and they will help you make the switch from other email service providers since they know they're a relatively new tool so that the friction of making a change is lessened.

Pros:

- Customizable forms and landing pages
- Visual automations and welcome sequences
- Subscriber tagging
- API support
- Free migration support for lists over 3,000
- Reporting
- Competitive pricing
- Great customer service

Cons:

- Reporting is somewhat limited right now, but they are working on adding more reports

Cost: Costs for most email service providers are dependent on the number of subscribers you have on your lists. ConvertKit's pricing is between $29 and $79 per month for up to 5,000 subscribers. For more than 5,000 subscribers, they'll put you on a custom plan that you can calculate on their pricing page.

Other email marketing tools to try:

- Mailchimp
- Infusionsoft

General Business Tools

GetFeedback https://www.getfeedback.com/

Wondering how your clients are feeling about you? Want to set up a survey of your audience? Or do you just need to know your team members' t-shirt sizes so you can send them something fun in the mail?

GetFeedback is a fun and intuitive tool for setting up feedback forms and surveys. We like it better than Google Forms or SurveyMonkey because it allows for some more advanced features, like email embedding and design customization. I also personally appreciate the design better than the other tools, although Typeform is another appealing option. The main reason we chose GetFeedback over Typeform was that it allows you to collect Net Promoter Score, which is important to us.

Pros:

- Easy form creation tool
- Embed into emails
- Track net promoter score
- Custom branding and colors
- Advanced logic and reporting for all forms
- Customizable templates
- Salesforce integration for higher paid plans
- Mobile-friendly surveys
- Website widgets and embed codes available for forms
- Mobile app

Cons:

- More expensive than other survey tools

Cost: 14-day free trial, then $50-$200+ per month for more advanced features.

Traveling Mailbox https://travelingmailbox.com/

Oh, Traveling Mailbox. I have a love/hate relationship with this tool. On the one hand, I love its functionality. On the other hand, I hate checking it. But that's why I'll have an assistant who can do that for me soon!

This tool has saved me from having to write my home address on important business and legal documents. And it saves me from receiving and opening mail. I hate receiving and opening mail.

How does it work? You're basically paying for an address in the city of your choice (New York City was my preferred location, which costs slightly more but is worthwhile) and someone to process your mail for you. When a letter comes in, you get an email. You can then request for them to open and scan the letter or forward it to an address of your choosing. I decide this based on what's inside the envelope. I always request the open and scan first, which is free. Then, if it's just a letter I download the PDF and file it in the appropriate place or print it. If it's a check or something where I need the original copy, I request the forward to my house for a small fee.

This way, I have digital copies of everything and only receive physical copies of mail or checks I actually need.

Pros:

- Affordable mail receipt service, especially if you are a digital nomad or work from home
- Quick open and scan services so you can see mail quickly
- Forwarding service for a small fee
- Simple to setup and use
- Choose from many different cities and address types
- Free mail shredding when you're done with the physical copies

Cons:

- Not available in all cities
- There is a lag time between the time the mail arrives and the time it lands in your Traveling Mailbox, so urgent items are better off going to your physical address
- Envelopes only, no packages
- You still have to check it!

Cost: Monthly fees start at $15 and go up to $55 depending on how much mail you receive and how many mailbox recipients you need to manage.

Quickbooks Online
https://quickbooks.intuit.com/online/

I always thought Quickbooks was too robust for my small business, but I've learned that's not the case. It's the financial tool of choice for most accountants, which was what prompted us to make the switch over from Freshbooks. It offers us the ability to not only send invoices and track expenses, but also to send purchase orders to contractors and track time spent on different clients and projects.

Quickbooks has great reports and is intuitive for the average, not-so-financially-savvy user to navigate. It does require some learning, but their knowledge base and support staff is generally very helpful. The way we've been able to integrate our bank accounts and credit cards, allow online payment from our clients, and share access with our accountants has been extremely helpful from a cash management and productivity perspective.

Pros:

- Common tool for many accountants to manage your books
- Easy to integrate bank accounts and credit cards for easy expense tracking
- Easy to set up recurring invoices and automatic reminders
- Easy to set up purchase orders for contractors
- Accept online credit card or bank payments
- Track inventory
- Track time
- Payroll services included with certain paid plans
- Integration with tools like Paypal, Square, and Shopify
- Mobile app

Cons:

- Requires a bit more of a learning curve than smaller tools like Freshbooks
- Can have glitches, such as sending invoices early, losing integration temporarily with credit card companies or banks, and accidentally sending reminders for invoices that have already been paid

Cost: Free trial for thirty days, then $10-$50 per month depending on the level of features you need. They run promotions often so you can usually find a lower price for a limited time if you keep your ear open for it.

Gusto https://gusto.com/

I've been using Gusto since the days when it was called ZenPayroll and have been a very happy customer from the beginning. Gusto is an easy, friendly payroll solution that allows you to pay both employees and contractors. They file the necessary paperwork with the government for you and allow each team member to set their own withholdings as they wish. At the end of year, each team member gets the appropriate W2 or 1099 form so you don't have to worry about putting things in the mail or calculating payments. Their customer service is excellent and they're very helpful when dealing with contractors across multiple states.

Pros:

- Easy, friendly payroll tool
- Pay contractors and employees

- Automatically generate end-of-year forms for team members
- Automatically files necessary paperwork with the federal and state government to keep you compliant
- Offers health insurance and workers comp options in certain markets
- Manages paid-time-off requests and other benefits
- Employees and contractors can easily change and manage their profiles
- Offers connections with certified accountants who can manage the tool for you

Cons:

- The benefits they offer are not available for all markets and for all team sizes

Cost: Free trial for one month, then $39 per month plus $6-12 per month per person depending the features you need. The highest level plan is $149 per month plus $12 per person per month.

ACKNOWLEDGMENTS

I've wanted to write this book for so long but was so afraid to do it because I was worried I would forget to thank someone in the acknowledgments section. Just kidding. (Although I'm sure I forgot someone.) This was a labor of love, something that I never actually thought I'd be able to do with all the pressures on my schedule and my brain. There were several people who calmed me down, took some of the burden of work off my plate, and simply believed in me enough to make this happen.

Mom, you were the first role model I had (besides Bette Midler!) and you continue to be the bright shining light in my life. Whenever I'm faced with adversity, I always think, "What would Karen do?" And my problems are solved. Thank you for being the best travel buddy, for always giving me honest advice, and for being my biggest inspiration to be the best possible version of myself. If I grow up to be half as respected, cherished, and accomplished as you are, I will call that a win!

Dad, you've shown me that anyone can be an artist and that "art" does not have only one definition. Your support of the arts has inspired me to keep writing and playing music. Your leadership of countless creatives and the lessons it has taught you have been absorbed by osmosis to me! Okay, not all of them, but at least some of them. And they have been invaluable as I grow my business and my confidence as a leader. Thank you.

Andy, you've put up with me through the very worst, and for that you deserve a medal. I never thought I'd end up with such a loving, generous, thoughtful, funny, smart, and incredibly kind man. Most days I don't feel like I deserve you, yet here we are planning a wedding! I'm so grateful to have someone who supports my every whim, tolerates my neuroses, and always knows how to help me take the breaks I need. Here's to many more years of champagne toasts for no other reason except because we're in love. Because that's something to celebrate.

Becca, you've been by my side, witnessing this little business grow into something that I never thought was possible, always with a smile on your face and a pun in your pocket. You've helped me become more emotionally intelligent (an ongoing battle), your WAHM status is an inspiration to moms and dads everywhere, and your contributions to the team and my life are invaluable. Thank you for being my sounding board, the level head I never had, and my biggest cheerleader.

Jenn, I'm so glad you pestered me into giving you a chance all those years ago. You deserved it. I knew you were going to do great things when I found myself giving you up as my own assistant so that you could serve our clients. You're a sponge for knowledge and it's been amazing watching you grow into our CCO over the years. You keep me and this entire business in line in more ways than one and I simply don't know where I would be without you. Thank you for pushing me when I need to be pushed, pulling us all toward achieving our biggest goals, and for not being afraid to be the bad cop when all I can do is be the good cop!

Ann, I still can't believe you were able to make the time to write the foreword for this book. Because I know how busy your schedule is and how many demands you have on your time, your words mean even more to me than you can imagine. I am so grateful to have gotten to know you so well over the years through our weekly calls, our pizza-making classes, our obsession with our dogs, and our conference-buddy hangouts. I think being in your presence helps me become a better writer, although I still have a long way to go. Your dedication to your craft, your "slow trumps fast" mentality, and your generous heart are a guiding light. Thank you for inspiring me, believing in me, and, perhaps most importantly, keeping me under your wing for all these years!

Amy, my sister from another mister! We both said we wanted to write books before we turned 30. Well, we didn't quite make that goal, but 31 and two weddings will have to do! Your success is such an inspiration for me, but what's more, you have always remained true to yourself and you've never let your own ego or anyone else's ideas get in your way. I look forward to many more years of success, adventure, and excitement with you. Thank you for being my friend, my champion, and my soul sister.

Jay, you actually trump Andy with the amount of time you have had to put up with me. Of course, you don't have to live with me so that makes things a little easier, I hope! You have always encouraged me to let my best self shine through, even when I didn't know who my best self was. You pushed me to challenge my assumptions about what I could do and handle, with a little tequila and chile rellenos on the side. I've become a better businesswoman, a better leader, and a better person as a result. I'm so grateful to call you a mentor and a friend. Thank you.

Lily, your passion and perseverance in everything you do has made me go, "Oh hell yeah!" on multiple occasions. Did you ever think our summer camp shenanigans would have led us to where we are today? I admire your work ethic, your cocktail-making skills, and your dedication to family and friends. We've been through so much, but I know that this is just the beginning of many more years of martinis and world domination! Maybe not in that order. Thank you.

Liz, I think our countless ideas for new businesses were what fueled the idea that I could run a business in the first place. I hope that one day our dreams of opening a music venue/coffee shop come true and until then, we can keep dreaming! I'm so lucky to have had you as a freshman year neighbor and so glad we have been able to remain close despite new jobs, new relationships, and new cities. Your infectious energy and passion for life keep me going. Thank you.

Elise, you continue to surpass my expectations with every project I throw at you. You embody the characteristics of an excellent virtual assistant and I wrote much of this book with you in mind. Thank you for always being great and thank you in particular for your help doing all the annoying formatting and technical tasks that allowed this book to be published so beautifully!

Matt, Karen, Janna, Dustin, and Non, I truly couldn't have done this without you. Your guidance, patience, and hard work helping me craft, edit, and promote this book have been invaluable. I'm so glad to have gotten to know you better personally and I look forward to collaborating professionally for years to come. Thank you.

Finally, I need to acknowledge the entire Don't Panic Management and Convince & Convert teams, past and present. Your hard work and dedication has helped power the engine that drives these businesses forward. I have learned something special from each and every one of you and you've helped me believe in the power of our work every day. Thank you for giving your all, for keeping a positive attitude even in the face of adversity, and for treating me not only as a colleague, but as a friend.

And if you made it this far, dear reader, thank you for being here. Please feel free to email me with any questions, comments, typos, or for my family's delicious pumpkin cheesecake recipe: jess@dontpanicmgmt.com

ABOUT THE AUTHOR

Jess Ostroff is a writer, speaker, and proud Director of Calm. Her company, Don't Panic Management, is the agency that embodies a people-first approach to virtual assistant success. Since 2011, she's been making the best possible matches between chaotic, overworked entrepreneurs and focused, calm virtual assistants. Offering services that span from administrative assistance to marketing support, she finds deep joy in making a difference through service. It's her goal to provide new, painless options for people to get work done as the future of virtual work becomes a reality.

When she's not speaking, writing, or researching productivity hacks, you can find Jess trying new recipes, popping champagne, searching the next great music festival to attend, or playing with her labradoodle, Hummus.

INVITE JESS TO SPEAK AT YOUR NEXT EVENT

Jess loves connecting great ideas with tangible action plans. She has spoken at private company retreats, large industry conferences, and traveling conventions around the world. Topics include:

- 7 Next-Level Strategies to Save Your Sanity Through Outsourcing
- A 10-Step Framework to Get Your Projects Done On Time Every Time
- Stop Creating Accidental Content
- Why the Future is Virtual (But Not the Way You Think)
- How to Find, Hire, and Train the Best Virtual Assistant for You

. . . and much more! Get in touch to book Jess for one of these topics or work with her to create a custom presentation for your audience. Keynote and workshop options are available for 2018 and beyond.

http://jessostroff.com/speaking

Made in the USA
Columbia, SC
30 April 2018